FRACTURED COMMUNITIES:
Dissecting the Ripple Effects of Gun Violence

Dear Sureya,
Hope you'll find some useful gems within these pages.
Rev. Sky

Rev. Sky Starr

Copyright © 2021 Rev. Sky Starr

All rights reserved. No portion of this book may be reproduced, stored in a retrieval system, or transmitted in any form or by any means - electronic, mechanical, photocopy, recording, scanning, or other - except for brief quotations in critical reviews, articles, or groups, without written permission of the author/publisher. Send inquires to www.higherhealingcounselling.com

Published by Higher Healing Counselling Services
Fractured Communities: Dissecting the Ripple Effects of Gun Violence
Starr, Rev. Sky
ISBN 978-1-7778352-3-1 (Paperback)
ISBN 978-1-7778352-1-7 (eBook)
ISBN 978-1-7778352-0-0 (Hardcover
ISBN 978-1-7778352-2-4 (Audio)

Edited by Melissa McLeod
Book production by Dawn James, Publish and Promote
Cover design by Publish and Promote.
Book layout and interior design by Perseus Design
Illustrations by: Jay Starr

Printed and bound in Canada.

Every reasonable effort has been made to trace ownership of copyright materials. Information enabling the author to rectify any reference or credit in future printings will be welcomed.

Note to the reader: The information is provided for educational purposes only. In the event you use any of the information in this book for yourself, which is your constitutional right, the author and publisher assume no responsibility for your actions.

Dedicated to

Angel Mothers

I dedicate this book to the many brave survivor-mothers and other victims and survivors of gun violence, who allowed me to wade in the deep waters of grief and gun-related trauma with them, and who taught me to recognize the vastness of human resilience in harmony with community.

I'm unceasingly humbled by the trust, sincerity, and confidence these 'trauma troopers' placed in me.

Contents

Foreword 9

Acknowledgements 15

Introduction 19

    Declaration of Intent   21

    Reactionary Measures   22

    Unique Niche   23

    A Multifaceted Issue   24

    The Epidemic of Gun Violence   25

    Conclusion   26

PART ONE: COMMUNITY GRIEF 29

Chapter 1: Realities of Communal Grief 31

    Epidemiology of Gun Violence   38

The Human Face and Voice of Grief	39
Summary	42

Chapter 2: The Gatekeepers 45

Youth-Centric Prevention-Intervention Methods	50
Grief/Trauma and Tentacles	51
Summary	56

Chapter 3: Community's Maze 59

The Paradox of Connectivity and Brokenness	63
The Necessity of Wallowing	65
Summary	68

PART TWO: RECOGNITION AND VALIDATION OF COMMUNITY TRAUMA 71

Chapter 4: Grief-Related Trauma 79

Perpetrators and Associates	79
Legacies of Trauma	82
Summary	85

Chapter 5: Needs Assessment 87

Necessary Time and Space	89
Holding Space	91
Freshman Griever	93
Summary	95

Chapter 6: Getting a Grip on Grief 97

Psychological Upheaval	100
Gun Violence Education & Grief/Trauma Education	102
Putting Emotions in Perspective	104

Contents

Sadness and Depression	105
Panic, Fear, and Anxiety	107
Guilt, Regret, and Blame	108
Explosive Emotions	110
Relief and Release	112
Crying is OK Here!	115
Measuring and Comparing Grief	118
Understanding Gun Violence and Grief/Trauma Education	123
Parental Foresight	128
Summary	129

PART THREE: RELUCTANT TRAVELLERS 131

Chapter 7: Cultural Sensitivity: Age, Gender, Trauma, and Culture 135

Cultural Sensitivity in Trauma	137
Stigmatization with Ramification	143
Along the Zig-Zag Path	145
Summary	147

Chapter 8: Meaning-Making & Legacies 149

Sharing Your Personal Journey	154
Constructing Legacies	157
Summary	160

Chapter 9: Reconciled Implementation 161

When Life Doesn't Make Sense	163
Where Do I Fit in?	165
Summary	168

PART FOUR: HOLISTIC OVERVIEW 171

Chapter 10: Community and Invisible Wounds 175
- Physical Reactions — 181
- Emotional Reactions — 183
- Cognitive Reactions — 184
- Behavioural Reactions — 186
- Spiritual Reactions — 187
- Deserved Acknowledgement — 189
- Grievers' Beatitudes — 189
- Spirituality — 191
- Protracted Journey — 193
- Crisis of Faith — 194

Chapter 11: Honouring Our Grief 201
- Extinguishing Closure — 205
- Grief Languages — 210

Chapter 12: Prolonged Grief 215
- Cold cases — 218
- Rare Justice — 220
- Recommendations and Conclusion — 221

Closing Commentary - Ardene, Robinson Vollman 231
Glossary of Terminology 235
References 261

Foreword

Annette Bailey, PhD
Ryerson University, Toronto, Canada

THIS BOOK IS A FUSION of conviction, struggles, and commitment towards the ideals of community healing. Within the pages of this book, Rev. Sky Starr demonstrates her commitment to the healing of communities. As a community advocate and trauma specialist, her work exemplifies the ideology that community healing is a natural part of community development. For racialized communities devastated by gun violence exposure, death, and injuries, this development is wrapped up in the politics of race that hampers community healing.

The modern politics of gun violence, primarily related to race and criminality, takes away from the social and psychological impacts of gun violence on individuals, families, and communities. Rev. Starr compels us to re-examine, reframe, and redefine the issue of gun violence from a humanistic perspective, by settling on the heart of the matter—the traumatic impact of violence on communities. She challenges us to think of the centrality of the impacts on affected communities, and calls attention to the urgency for social change.

In essence, readers are invited to expand their views and empathy beyond the 'gun' and the 'shooter' to understand the complexities of social and psychological factors that compound the experiences of community violence. This holds incredible comfort for me as a mother, nurse, public practitioner, and educator who has, for over 10 years, conducted research to better understand the survivorship experiences of victims and survivors of gun violence.

My understanding of gun violence is that it is a complex phenomenon. Deeply entrenched socio-political and psychological factors, tightly intersected without pattern or predictability, make gun violence complex. While gun violence is complex, its unbendable persistence is not merely a matter of its obscurities but rather the diminished private and public sector support afforded to this issue. Most revealing is the fact that gun violence prevention is not integrated into a public health framework.

If framed as a public health priority, gun violence can receive the same coordinated public health attention as other deadly and debilitating issues, such as the COVID-19 pandemic. If supported within public health principles of community capacity building, partnership and collaboration, advocacy, and social equity, community healing from gun violence can be achieved.

But sobering conversations with Black mothers who lose children to gun violence and Black youth who lose multiple friends and family members have shown that gun violence in Toronto's Black communities is far from receiving necessary and consistent public health support. The racial stigma attached to gun violence is continuing to stifle social and political commitment and response.

Foreword

Gun violence is the greatest threat to the lifespan, safety, and growth of young Black males in Canada's urban neighbourhoods. There are no moments of reprieve from burying and mourning the lives and legacies of Black sons and fathers in these neighbourhoods. Their deaths leave a sweltering cloud of grief and trauma that steals hopes and dreams from friends and families. Friends and siblings of Black youth killed by gun violence are propelled into early experiences of trauma without trauma support. With frequent and compounding deaths, trauma responses are exacerbated, resulting in negative outcomes for entire families.

The historical devaluing of Black bodies and lives makes it not only easier for Derek Chauvin to stop George Floyd's breath with a knee on his neck, but for the growing gun deaths of Black youth in Toronto's Black communities to appear trivial. Increased attention to Black-on-Black shootings has deliberately masked the significance of social disparities, systemic oppression, and anti-Black racism in these deaths.

When gun violence is seen as a problem only within Black communities and not as a socially created problem, the deaths of young Black sons and fathers are blamed on deficiencies in parenting, rather than social inequities. The growing demise of Black boys and men to gun violence threatens generational structures of growth and leadership in Black communities. Rev. Starr spotlights the profound truth that when the structures of families and communities are fractured by gun violence, the promise of a whole generation is weakened.

Black mothers are the pillars of Black families. When they are emotionally weakened by the sudden and traumatic death of their children to gun violence, the family function suffers. Black mothers' stories are those of complicated grief and trauma, prolonged depression, job loss, diminished social and system supports/services, and suicidal ideation. Although there are stories of resilience, Black mothers' resilience process is far from simple. It is navigated and negotiated within the racial and social complications that accompany their survivorship experiences.

Gun violence grief stifles the meaningful contribution that Black mothers can make to their families and communities. No home can stand strong when a pillar is broken, and by extension, no society can stand strong when families are broken. The interplay of gun violence stigma and racism creates profound and prolonged trauma for Black communities, which snuffs out the potential legacies, excellence, and creativity from these communities.

Rev. Starr's recommendation for culturally appropriate and accessible trauma-informed care for Black families and communities, comes from a long history of observing the lack of social recognition of the debilitating consequences of unattenuated gun violence trauma in these communities.

The psychological scars of gun violence trauma are not discussed to any significant degree in the literature. What the public knows about gun violence is what they hear from media reports, which is never comprehensive of causes, impacts and experiences. Therefore, the suffering of economically disadvantaged communities is often invisible.

The invisible scars of community gun violence are facilitated by negative public opinion and decreased social empathy, with blame inflicted on these communities. In highlighting the trauma realities of gun violence, Rev. Starr humanizes the struggles of these communities. The struggles aren't just ideological; they shape people's lives, growth, and aspirations.

Healing for communities fractured by gun violence can mean many things, but what is central is the ability for families to thrive and for communities to work agreeably with social institutions for social change. Disadvantaged neighbourhoods should never be separated in their experiences with violence or have to rely on their limited resources to adjust to what seems like a never-ending, ever-enduring fight to be free of gun violence.

Rev. Starr's thoughts, experiences, and expertise speak to social responsibility for the suffering of communities fractured by gun violence; a collective transformation in the worldview of leaders and decision-makers who have the power to facilitate change; the human value of Black lives taken by guns and loved ones left to grieve their loss; and importantly, the social deconstruction of the social injustice walls that block reconciliation, and a culture of peace around gun violence.

For its role in interrupting legacies of pain in communities affected by violence, this book isn't just timely; it is essential.

Dr. Annette Bailey, RN, BScN, MSN, PhD is a professor at Ryerson University. She specializes in health promotion, education and research in gun violence survivorship, including traumatic stress and resilience among survivors of community and interpersonal violence.

ACKNOWLEDGEMENTS

This book emanated in the murky waters of traumatic pain while witnessing heart-wrenching suffering over 17 years. Working with mothers, children, families, and communities has been an enriching, though difficult journey. Formulation of this work was conceived by nudging comments from supporters, which reminded me of the absence of information on gun violence and the reactionary floundering which followed every incident without fail.

    I distinctly remember feeling the massive weight of responsibility after my first crisis response. Even though I felt academically equipped, with knowledge from required education to become a therapist; with practicing mock trials on colleagues at our skills lab for six months; with the required hours of face-to-face counselling with an experienced supervisor and clients to become accredited. Despite the 'know-how,' sitting in the throes of intense, primary suffering required a significant paradigm shift. Although the effect was similar to my first patient in my 19-year nursing career, my mind and reasoning knew they could not be paralleled.

Questions swirled and taunted before the humane response surfaced. Was I ready to take on this task? Would I be able to provide the emotional support that these families deserve? The need was insurmountable, no doubt. But the care was more than a necessity. It was desperately needed and should be a priority. Witnessing the enormity of pain from the first mother and immediate family I served, cemented my resolve to be as competent, compassionate and thorough as every family deserved.

I am indebted to the many mother-survivors who trusted me and graciously allowed me to wade in the sweltering waters of fresh trauma with them, exposing their most vulnerable selves and situations with me. And I am humbled and appreciative to the victims and survivors of gun violence who invited and included me on their journey of healing and rediscovery of self. I'm especially obliged to the children and youth who included me in their lives—albeit by default—but whose innocence and bravado taught me irreplaceable lessons in human tenacity.

Community's blended dichotomy of belonging and disgrace, cohesiveness and shame, has been starkly contrasted among the multitude of traumatic needs following a gun violence death. Yet, I continue to be encouraged by residents in various communities who willingly share their time and resources when needed. Volunteers within communities merge their time, talents, and synergy to assist victims and survivors, and I'll be forever beholden to them.

Over 17 years of intense, fatiguing, but important stories are weaved into this work, including many promptings from mothers who encouraged me to put truth to words. In actuality, this book was envisioned in early 2010, but continual responses to gun violence and the ongoing needs of survivors hindered an earlier publication. Despite its being long-overdue, I'm a firm believer

Acknowledgements

in the adage that *'nothing happens before its time.'* Time nurtures creativity; time produces actualization; and time teaches, notifies, and makes things and situations materialize to their fullest reality.

Humanity is made to recognize the incredible loss of lives and human dignity amid the continuous loss of young lives to gun violence. Over time, I've been privileged to learn from and rub shoulders with like-minded folks who share my concerns for gun violence victims and survivors.

Dr. Annette Bailey is one such individual who realized and shared my passion for acquiring empirical data to assist and better treat those afflicted by gun violence trauma. We met, conversed, and wrote frequently. Her collaboration in our struggle to source funding, conduct research, and document findings has furthered our work and emphasized the need for structural investigation; of how disenfranchised grief continues to plague marginalized communities.

Partners, collaborators, and supporters (who can't all be named) aided programs, events, and activities that supported survivors. They, too, deserve applause for their resourcefulness and kind accommodation to the complexities of supporting repetitive trauma in communities.

I owe recognition and considerable gratitude to my church family, who volunteered their time, who gave from whatever they had, and who travelled with me to crisis sites. From a social mandate standpoint, their prayers for my safety and their "check-ins" were a source of comfort and encouragement when exhaustion threatened to overwhelm me.

Words are inadequate to fully express profound gratitude to my family, whose support and love sustained my endeavours to provide competent, consistent services in communities across the GTA (greater Toronto area).

My husband, Jay, became my predominant supporter and willingly gave from his small business when my resources were spent. He contributed the majority of administrative supplies needed for Out Of Bounds, the charitable organization I founded to eradicate gun violence and its trauma. Not only did he believe in what I strived to do, but he also completed our 10-week training session and became a trained facilitator who chauffeured me and assisted during new crises.

Jay listened attentively during conversations and acted swiftly by providing supplies that were lacking. I've since learned to curtail my needs within his hearing range to not deplete his resources. Most importantly, he continues to encourage me and provide personal care when I need to regain equilibrium. My younger son, Rowan, became my editor, who scrutinized articles, letters, and documents and provided constructive criticism where necessary. He, too, became a trained facilitator and volunteer, filling in when I needed a performer or hands-on work.

Lastly, my older son, Al. St. Louis is our reigning in-house moderator, who shared his talented craft of spoken word, and magnetism, hosting our Fathers Across Cultures Gala from its inception in 2009.

I give praise for all the above blessings and divine insights, grace and strength to assist others in an area deprived of adequate attention and support. This book is a glimpse of the varying escapades gleaned from myriads of ongoing gun violence episodes.

Introduction

Gun violence has mushroomed in recent years, creating havoc in communities, countries, and on an alarmingly global scale. This is predominantly true for marginalized communities where systemic issues and health determinants equally plague residents. While the increase in gun-related deaths continues to impede the safety of communities and diminish mental wellbeing, the overall cost to society is the steady detriment of affected ethnicity.

Canada has long prided itself as a tolerant nation with claims of being a safe, non-violent, and inclusive country. Yet, the repeating occurrences of gun-violent deaths result in injuries to innocent Canadians, decreased safety in numerous communities, and premature loss of lives.

Maslow's hierarchy of needs highlights safety and security among its foundational tools as a basic human need. The Ottawa Charter for Health Promotion, (1986), complements Maslow's categorized assembly, emphasizing advocacy of promotion of health in all appropriate forums, which would support countries in setting up strategies and programs towards that objective (Ottawa Charter, 1986).

Sudden, traumatic gun violence deaths have bombarded mothers and their families during the last two decades. Statistic Canada reports a 38% increase in gun-related deaths in 2019, listing Toronto as experiencing a dramatic increase in gun homicide. Additionally, handguns are the primary weapon used in gun-related deaths. Most distressing for victims and survivors is the massive gap in services to manage the sudden losses, drastic disruption in everyday activities, and the lifelong stressors accompanying such emotionally traumatic upheaval.

Another complicated setback is the secondary losses that follow the initial loss. Those who have jobs don't easily bounce back from the sudden trauma which manifests in physical ailments hindering their return to normalcy. Survivors frequently suffer from multiple conditions and symptoms such as headaches, depression, insomnia, hypervigilance, flashbacks, memory loss, and hypertension, to name a few.

Grieving is distinct for each person, and no 'one-size-fits-all' process can be used for healing. Structured trauma-focused debriefing must be strategically facilitated within a safe space to promote wellness. Healing gun violence trauma requires a unique model of care that combines education and prevention/intervention measures with a trauma-focused, evidence-based, and customized approach (Starr, 2015).

Such a model must be developed from working side-by-side with gun violence grievers, tailored to individual, group, and community care. This multi-pronged approach should be established in collaboration with the federal, provincial, and municipal governments, accompanied by specific input from caregivers directly associated with those affected by gun violence trauma, with deep community involvement.

Introduction

Declaration of Intent

The chief intent of this book is to raise awareness of the devastation that surrounds gun violence and the lasting, traumatic effects for unsuspecting children, youth, families, and plague-ridden communities. This dreaded, lethal foe incessantly diminishes hopes and dreams, robbing youth—particularly young men of living—who faintly express the desire to see their eighteenth birthday.

Additional goals are to spark and instill renewed hope—for youth who live in fear for their lives every day; for siblings, mothers, fathers, and families who are barely surviving with the shadow of death as a dark shroud over their heads; for frontline workers who detect the helplessness that permeates young lives; and, for healthcare workers and facilitators who bear the brunt of dealing with ongoing issues of traumatic grief.

For empathizers who might not understand how challenging and dangerous life is for marginalized communities, we earnestly expect that this information will provide an *'eagles-eye view'* of the everyday situations experienced by those who are 'underprivileged.'

More significantly, the hope is that this compilation will stir hearts to 'see' the human faces of grief, loss, and trauma and create a platform for open dialogue where victims and survivors can be validated and enabled; and where agencies, communities, facilitators, and practitioners can find mutual alliance. Ultimately, I'm optimistic that a foundational platform can be established so that public health interests and policymakers can unite with communities, by working to enhance people's wellbeing and reduce the health risks associated with gun violence trauma. (Charter, 1986).

Reactionary Measures

On an individual and communal level, desensitization is a by-product of the repetitive occurrences of gun violence. It has become common for residents, including children and youth, to show little or no emotions when hearing about another shooting death.

The general expectation is that most people would have an organic response to grief and loss. However, gun violence trauma, over time, has cultivated a *reactive* response rather than a proactive one.

Many people will show up after a fatal shooting, visit the family, express customary condolences, and even attend the vigil, funeral, and 'after gathering' of a recent victim of gun violence. In recent years, many have viewed these practices as folks 'going through the motions.' Public officials make it a point to show up with well-intentioned words and phrases for family, community, and hopes of the media reaching the wider community.

Now, these responses are viewed as mundane and stagnant. Communities yearn for a more pre-emptive approach to crisis response rather than the primitive reactionary appearances. Mothers aren't pacified with pleasantries and well-wishes; youth mistrust that others care about their wellbeing; residents parallel what might be well-intentioned concerns as superficial, expecting the same incidents to reoccur. There needs to be a concerted effort to include and engage the community with positive, significant, holistic actions to curb the systemic issues that perpetuate frustration, encourage marginalization, and promote violence.

Introduction

Unique Niche

Supporting children, youth, mothers, families, and communities through trauma has been a focal point of my life for almost 20 years. What I've learned is that traumatic reactivity symptoms trickle from the emotional, physical, intellectual, psycho-social and, of course, spiritual levels. And each person's reaction to grief, loss, and trauma is as unique to an individual as their fingerprints.

My specific area of expertise is creating customized, practical solutions that individuals can apply within their journey with grief and trauma. Acquired experience stems from responding to gun violence, sitting within the anguish of fresh, complicated, and traumatic grief alongside children, youth, mothers, families, and communities.

After 'the Year of the Gun' in 2005, I founded, Out Of Bounds: Grief and Trauma Support, a registered charitable organization focusing on providing care for gun violence trauma. Over the years, I created customized programs and groups, working extensively to provide trans-cultural post-care to address the emotional distress of gun violence. I recruited and trained volunteers, professionals, and those who seek to support survivors of violence.

We researched and collected empirical data from victims and survivors of gun violence in partnership with scholars from Ryerson University and funding from the Women's College Hospital. Utilizing participatory action research (PAR) methods, we identified gaps in services and pinpointed areas of specific needs by listening to mothers and those affected by gun violence. Seasonal training sessions that I design and teach, offer introductory, intermediary, and advanced level trauma-focused training to those who earnestly seek to respond to crises and support victims and survivors.

Among the hallmark of successful ventures, our Annual Community Interfaith Remembrance, now in its thirteenth year, commemorates all grievers while paying special attention to mothers who have lost a child or children to gun violence and other traumatic circumstances. These events draw attendees from all levels of government, the Greater Toronto Area (GTA) and other communities across Canada, and internationally from New York and Australia.

One marvels at the openness of people stricken with fresh trauma. They accept those around them who may or may not have experienced such excruciating emotional pain and graciously embrace the well-intentioned comfort that individual presence conveys during these passionate disruptions. I'm forever humbled by the trust, sincerity, and confidence these *'trauma troopers'* place in me.

A Multifaceted Issue

Grief-related trauma is intense and multi-faceted. It seeps into every area of human existence, penetrates all aspects of human functioning, and disrupts emotions. Gun-related trauma presents a wide range of reactions on the emotional, intellectual, physical, psycho-social, and spiritual levels that should be anticipated, authenticated, and treated.

As data continues to emerge from Stats Canada reporting the annual increase in gun injuries and death, Canadians and communities impatiently await the collective efforts of government and health officials.

Evolving interest in the psychological impact of traumatic grief is gaining traction, anticipating endorsed consolidation from policymakers and the much-needed alliance with community liaisons, to adequately create long-term, constructive, prevention/

intervention solutions to address gun violence. Such collaboration can fuel an expected response to promote health through concrete and effective community action in setting priorities, making decisions, planning strategies, and implementing them to achieve better health (Charter, 1986).

The Epidemic of Gun Violence

An undercurrent of covert consensus recognizes that gun violence is an epidemic. Decades of accelerated gun violence occurrences, injuries, and deaths tell the blatant tale. In their 'Position Statement,' the National Police Federation detailed their support for an evidence-based approach to advancing public safety and preventing gun violence in Canada (2020). Despite varying reluctance to declare gun violence an epidemic, constant invasions of this dreaded foe with subsequent deaths decry the plight of racialized communities.

In recent years, the Diagnostic and Statistical Manual of Mental Health (DSM-5) has concurred with mental health practitioners, listing depression as one of the main symptoms of traumatic grief, in acknowledging gun-related trauma as complicated grief (CG). Symptoms of CG are associated with, and predictive of substantial morbidity—depression, suicidal ideation, and high blood pressure, where adverse health behaviours are identified.

As communities continue to be plagued by the epidemic of gun violence and its aftermath, advocacy for competent services with policymakers is desperately needed. Consistent support through proactive responses, education, prevention/intervention measures, research, and creative approaches to funding, remains at the forefront of community requirements.

Conclusion

Mahatma Gandhi aptly indicated that *"A nation's greatness is measured by how it treats its weakest members."* Nothing weakens a child, a youth, a family, or a community more than having to repeatedly bury its future.

Knowledge has always been a motivational factor in raising human consciousness. We cannot 'un-know' what is imprinted on our minds or part of our everyday experience. We cannot 'un-know' that the consequences of gun violence linger for all of one's lifetime. Veronica Roth attested that 'Knowledge is power. Power to do evil ... or power to do good.'

Humanity's charge is to:

> *"Do all the good you can,*
> *By all the means you can,*
> *In all the ways you can,*
> *In all the places you can,*
> *At all the times you can,*
> *To all the people you can,*
> *As long as ever you can."*
> - John Wesley, Goodreads

Gun violence has irrefutably exploded in our communities, provinces, and throughout our country. It is distressing to verify that it has now become a global issue. The overall effects of gun-related grief, loss, violence, and trauma among youth, families, and communities are an ever-present health detriment.

Preventing, diminishing, and eventually eradicating gun violence is a complex problem requiring the organized cooperation of stakeholders on the federal, provincial, municipal, and communal levels. A holistic, evidence-based approach to address youth violence and gun-related trauma is warranted to ensure all interventions are directed to those most vulnerable, starting with children, youth, and families.

Therefore, as "…cultures within which people grieve continue to evolve and demand sensitivity…," (Strobe et al., p. 764), stakeholders' responses must also include understanding with action; knowing with implementation; and detection with tailored strategies that would educate, empower, and heal, while limiting stakeholders' negligence.

PART ONE

COMMUNITY GRIEF

CHAPTER 1

REALITIES OF COMMUNAL GRIEF

Just as ripples spread out when a single pebble is dropped into water, the actions of individuals can have far-reaching effects.
- Dalai Lama

COMMUNAL GRIEF, LIKE GENERALIZED GRIEF, will forever permeate human lives. Many feel inept in dealing with the principle of natural growth and development, which conveys the certainty that every living thing will eventually die. Yet, we tread and live within a thin line where life intertwines with death at every step.

Dating back to the medieval ages, death is a foe humanity dreads, doesn't understand, and has difficulty accepting. *The Black*

Death was the name given to a disease called the 'bubonic plague,' rampant during the Fourteenth Century. Historical records assessed that 1.5 million people out of an estimated 4 million people died between 1348 and 1350 because of the *"Black Death"* (Crawford, 2018). The level of fear, deaths, and social upheaval associated with the plague terrified villages and towns (Georgi, 2020). Similarly, emotions of foreboding and uncertainty related to gun deaths parallel those from the black plague.

Each person is born with an innate ability to grieve, to mourn automatically. A baby instinctively cries when they are uncomfortable or experience discomfort. Children intuitively wail from a scraped knee. Although teenagers appear 'macho,' they share grieved emotions with their 'homies.' During adulthood, emotions become catalogued into sadness, emotional pain, and depression. As human beings, we release pent-up emotions through tears, which help us express our sadness and allow others to know how or what we feel. Tears of pain, sorrow, and mourning are universally recognized throughout the various stages of life and human experience.

Today, gun violence closely equates to the chaos of the Middle Ages. With each devastatingly traumatic and life-altering effect, gun violence has reinstated a *"Black Death"* within communities with lethal force. This frequent, unrestrained violence creates proverbial ripple effects that permeate entire communities and beyond their borders.

Trauma associated with gun violence loss has wide-range effects that cascade to the entire community with three common and inconceivable elements. First, it creeps into lives and communities as an unexpected and intrusive visitor that one must entertain, albeit reluctantly and for some neighbourhoods, unavoidably. Secondly, the arrival of a gun violent death is so unexpectedly astonishing that one can never anticipate or prepare for it. Third, no person, family, or community, can even plan to prevent it from happening. The abruptness of gun violence ushers the unnatural, torrential overflow of shock, anguish, denial coupled with psychological and psycho-social distresses.

The ripple effect theory, coined by Jacob Kounin (1970), was used to demonstrate that the Iraq War became more personalized for people who knew or heard about soldiers killed or injured in Iraq (Duke, 2007). Using the ripple effect allegory, the article suggests that public opinion was swayed from that minor ripple effect, making the war personal on those two levels. Gun violence creates a devastatingly lasting ripple effect that penetrates nuclear and extended families, communities, neighbouring cities, nations, global ethnicities, and societies. Like a tsunami, the associated impacts of gun violence reverberate for entire lifetimes.

Death associated with gun violence, and the trauma it carries, is never a self-contained incident. Every instance of a gun-related death creates a tidal wave of grief and trauma manifested through a tri-tiered effect of suffering from prolonged ringlets of extended ripples. The most crushing impacts begin with members of the nuclear family, who are brutally affected. Mothers, fathers, siblings, grandmothers, grandfathers, and extended relatives must accept and endure the gruelling, fresh pangs of grief and trudge through a life-long journey to recovery.

On the secondary level, friends, peers, classmates, colleagues, club members, and acquaintances are affected. Community patrons, caregivers, church members, as well as perpetrators and their mothers, and the wider community are also secondary victims and survivors. Neighbouring communities and other provinces are equally and adversely affected as periphery victims.

First responders, health care providers, frontline workers, and social service workers are generally among the overlooked population who are also psychologically wounded within the concentric rippling circles of secondary victimization. Although usually disregarded, they too are touched by an array of mental, economic, and psycho-social problems from the outer stratum of the ripple.

Mothers who are considered stabilizers in single-parent families suffer a profound magnitude of effects. But these impacts are not just isolated within the affected families. Considered as a notorious "pebble in the pond," the sudden, traumatic death of a loved one from gun homicide ushers in a sequence of emotional, intellectual, physical, economic, and spiritual ailments that expand beyond time, space, and imagination (Starr & Bailey, 2017). An explosive act at its core, gun violence's "boulder-like" impact ricochets into the human spirit with decisive and volatile precision.

Figuratively, scientists, physicists, and meteorologists attest that ripples do not extend beyond the water's boundaries. They further claim that ripples are not dominant nor powerful enough to influence the pattern of water. (Staughton, 2020; Lynch, 2013). A familiar phrase in Quantum physics parallels ripples to sunsets, with the adage that they 'look pretty, but are temporary.'

In stark contrast, gun violence ripples are grotesque from the onset, with an increasing succession of life-long waves of the most profound psychological wounds, repeated through everyday happenings. Memory evokes painful triggers, such as saying or hearing the lost child's name or simply being in the home where they must walk past that child's room. Mothers and families are continuously re-traumatized by media reports of other shootings.

Unlike the water-ripple, gun homicide trauma surpasses the comparison. It supersedes the water's edge in terms of degree in emotional pain, rate of traumatic effects, and quantity of lives affected. The intensity and invasion of gun violence can only be equalled to the bubonic plague in reach, impact, and longevity.

Ongoing research in Toronto, Canada, indicates that at least 135 people are harmfully affected from one incident of gun violence death. Cause and effect functions in tandem with the ripple effects, emphasizing the excruciating truth that acts of gun violence create life-altering and extensive psychological trauma. Consequently, victims and survivors endure life-long detriments of which they cannot hope to overcome fully.

At its 2006 Council Session of the Geneva Declaration (GD), the World Health Organization (WHO) defined gun violence as:

> The intentional use of physical force or power, threatened or actual, against oneself, another person, or against a group or community that either results in or has a high likelihood of resulting in injury, death, psychological harm, mal-development, or deprivation.

The Geneva Declaration on Armed Violence and Development is a diplomatic initiative to address the interrelations between armed violence and development. More than 740,000 men, women, and children die each year because of armed violence. It's been editorially revised in 2005, 2006, and amended in 2017 to include the clause "respect to the patient, the community and the environment."

Despite WHO's intent to "support states and civil society actors to achieve measurable reductions in the global burden of armed violence in conflict and non-conflict settings by 2015" (GD, 2006), communities are experiencing a global epidemic-type surge in gun-violent deaths. Following its adoption and subsequent Editorial Revision, 173rd Council Session, of the Geneva Declaration in 2006, 42 countries enlisted. The GD has since endorsed 100 states due to the alarming amounts of homicide, gendercide, and community fatalities.

In previous years, the prevalence of gun violence was associated with disadvantaged and marginalized communities. This also brought a stigma to those communities where the mention of gun violence inferred conclusive assumptions of particular neighbourhoods. Recent episodes of gun violence are harshly marked by random attacks, which demonstrates no specific area or community. Whereas particular neighbourhoods were stigmatized with the dreaded "gun violence area" title, every region in the City of Toronto and across Canada is now experiencing gun violence, and with it, the trauma that ensues.

Nothing robs a community of hope more than a young life lost to gun violence. With each episode of gun violence, communities encounter tumultuous amounts of desolation, heart-rending pain, isolation, ongoing fears, and retraumatization. Realized threats from straying bullets coupled with uncertainty amid eminent dangers limit their productivity and erode the safety and security necessary for all humanity. Yet where they live is *home*. Though scorched by gun violence and stigma, this is their community.

Among the numerous associated effects of gun violence, advocates and communities voice their ongoing concerns that repeated exposure to gun violence creates a cycle of violence. Psychological effects such as anger and dissociation, desensitization to violence, and an increased likelihood of violence to resolve problems or express emotions are amid the lasting properties. Regrettably, communities fear that these cries fail to receive the necessary attention from city officials, health officials, politicians, and policymakers.

Marginalized communities pay an exorbitant price when gun violence is embedded within their structure. Safety and security, listed as a basic psychological need among Maslow's hierarchy of needs, is elusive and a rare commodity (Maslow, 1943).

Researchers cite many contributing factors which affect and trap families in cycles of violence and cry for alternatives to traditional treatment that would benefit adolescents and families within communities. Bagarrozzi (1998) and others stated that the combination of social isolation, scarcity of services, poor education and poverty puts these families at risk (Farrington, 1980) and heightens the probability that they will resort to physical violence as a means for resolving conjugal problems (Gelles, 1972; Marsden, 1978).

Sudden violent deaths, like any significant disaster, plague and affect communities for lengthy periods. Norris, F. H (2006) aptly states that "These negative effects ignite a chronic and periodically escalated alarm and shock [families within a community to periods of] complexity, and difficulty." He believed that the endless task of recovery, with sharply limited personal stamina, significantly increases family needs and deteriorates the effectiveness of community resources.

> "Such violence appears to have the greatest impact on mental health when harm and death are intentional; they are particularly hard for survivors to accept knowing that another human being inflicted the damage, causes us more mental anguish than "an accident" or the faceless, non-human forces of nature, where there is no one to blame or be accountable" (p. 36).

Critically, for communities where the perpetrator has been identified, these incidents create a phenomenon with a different life, where youth, families, and communities all play by different survival rules. Those privileged with information about these "human-caused disasters" feel the need to shield that knowledge in an uncanny code of silence that knits friend to friend, family to their rigid boundaries, and community members to silent suffering and fear.

Recent studies corroborate with Garbarino (2002, 2019), indicating that exposure to gun violence can also desensitize youth to the effects of violence and increase the likelihood that they will use violence as a means of resolving problems or expressing emotions.

Epidemiology of Gun Violence

With 50 percent of all homicides in Toronto committed with a gun, Toronto has the highest gun homicide rate among Canadian cities (Statistics Canada, 2011). Black youth aged 15-24 residing in marginalized neighbourhoods, with little income, resources, and support, are most vulnerable to be victims and survivors of gun violence (Janhevich, Bania, & Hastings, 2008; Statistics Canada, 2012).

These youth concurrently struggle with disenfranchised grief and trauma from losing multiple friends and family members to gun violence, exposing them to lifelong experiences with psychological disablement, and educational and social stagnation (Granek & Peleg-Sagy, 2015; Smith, 2015).

Recent research conducted with youth in Toronto who lost friends and families to gun violence revealed that trauma experienced by these youth had the strongest correlation to violence involvement; stronger than other variables assessed such as poverty, the type of neighbourhood they live in, unemployment, and education.

In conjunction with exposure to violence and loss, gun-related trauma shifts these youth's perspectives, behaviours, view of the world, and self, and informs how they grieve. Their social adjustment and ability to attain empowerment and build resilience are also hampered. The research indicated that the racial stigma of gun violence further complicates youth's grieving process, hinders their access to mental health support and perpetuates further involvement in gun violence attacks (Bailey, 2019, unpublished research).

Males between the ages of 15 and 24 are at a disproportionate risk of firearm injuries and constitute 94 percent of all firearm deaths. Stats Canada reported alarming rates of both suicide and homicide among that population. Data from 2008 to 2012 indicated 56 percent of firearm injuries and deaths among adolescents (ages 15 to 19), with homicide comprising 55 percent among young adults 20 to 24 years old (Sanders et al., 2017).

A startling understatement laces an unspoken understanding that gun violence could transpire at any time with dreadful circumstances. Kimhi & Shamai (2004), reported that one of the main risk factors on the physical, mental, emotional, and psychological responses during this period is the complication of overt and covert levels of political violence that many youths experience. Out Of Bounds (OOB) needs assessments done during 2006 and 2015 found that from a youth perspective, their lack of trust in the institutional systems leaves them little recourse in their choice to engage in gun violence.

The City of Toronto has had to contend with gun violence for the last 30 years. The year 2005 was dubbed the "Year of the Gun" after a startling accumulation of shooting deaths. Year 2018 was significantly different, not only with the alarming number of 482 shootings, [609 victims, 185 injuries, with 51 deaths], but rather the city's, and the country's, involuntary awareness of gun violence (CBC, 2019). OOB was precisely created to intercept and address gun violence, provide trauma-focused services to youth, families, schools, and communities, and raise awareness to this national issue that ought to concern every Canadian.

The Human Face and Voice of Grief

Grief assumes varying faces and characteristics. Although the 'faces' of grief generally relate to its manifestation in the lives of those affected, gun violence-related grief personifies the actual lives touched, the hearts affected, and the communities that bear the brunt of prolonged psychological trauma. Hopes and dreams are shattered; relationships are severed; loss of life equates to eventual loss of family systems; livelihood potentials become non-existent; but more significantly, the future of specific race(s) is steadily being erased.

Children are innocent and the most unwitting casualties of gun violence. Five-year-old children, or younger, who witness or hear gunshots, listen to conversations and attend funerals of loved ones are forever marred. Although their vocabulary and mentality are limited, many understand when something is wrong or when a brother, cousin, uncle, and dad suddenly disappears.

The most painful and challenging task is finding an appropriate answer for the child who witnesses the unfortunate demise of a loved one and asks, *"Why is ----- not moving? Why is he not getting up?"* Exposure to and witnessing gun violence has a profound and overwhelmingly lasting impact on children's psychological and mental wellbeing. It affects their educational performance, their ability to play and interact freely with others, and the surging psychological trauma lingers for life.

Lack of research on gun-related incidents involving children hinders responders and the community's ability to provide adequate support, since whatever limited information there is focuses on those who have died from gun violence.

A pioneer in the field of gun violence trauma, James Garbarino (2002), highlighted the lasting 'emotional scars' and traumatic effects that gun violence has on children and youth. He cited exposure at home and school to community occurrences and even violent media renditions as contributing factors. The absence of material surrounding gun violence is slowly being rectified with varying levels of peaked interest. Yet, restricted research, lack of empirical data, and fear hinder the progress to 'mitigate the effects of gun violence' that Garbarino solicits.

Dr. Natasha Saunders, a prominent doctor at The Hospital for Sick Children (SickKids) and lead author in a study during 2008 to 2012, claimed that a child or youth is injured by gun violence every day in Ontario, bringing focus to the enormity of gun-related issues for children and youth. This much-needed spotlight, focusing on children and youth of immigrant families, exposed how gun-related injuries substantially contribute to their morbidity and mortality (2017). Affirming the lack of gun-related data on children under 15, her report indicated 15 suicides, 10 homicides, 7 unintentional deaths daily, and 2 whose type (death) was undetermined.

The multifaceted issue of recovery for affected children would require analytical data collection, psychological and psycho-social treatment, and age-appropriate recovery tactics. Such an intentional approach needs to be conducted by experienced trauma-informed facilitators, who are not only sensitive to all the related data, but are well-versed in the inter-related systemic issues.

Adolescence has been described as "a transitional period in which individuals' experience major physical, cognitive, and socio-effective changes, compounded by family structure, and school accidental changes" (Dumont & Provost, 1999; Allen & Waterman, 2019). Regularity of adverse events, coupled with grief and loss amid these turbulent times, creates a higher panic and vulnerability for these youth.

A sense of helplessness is prevalent among their circles, for males and females alike. They try to make sense of, and place meaning to the increasingly chaotic and epidemic situation of recurrent deaths and losses. It is not uncommon for youth to express the woeful desire to 'see their eighteenth birthday.' With desired hope, a dichotomy of defenselessness forecasts a dismal future, where youth often succumb to the mirage of attaining a better life through dangerous activities.

Youth often share the sickening emotions that invade their minds like waves of familiar shock and pain. Siblings recount the dread they harbour, that it might be another member of their immediate family; they ruminate worrisome thoughts about the daily internal fear and impending pain that their mothers carry; youth voice the incessant fear of the 'unknown' day that someone would pound on their front door to relay alarming news of their demise.

And, within the community at large, residents exist from day to day, not knowing when another young life will be ripped from the community's fabric because of gun violence, and launch a new phase of traumatic ripples.

Summary

In their 2020 report, WHO (World Health Organization) listed homicide as the fourth leading cause of death worldwide among 15-29-year-olds. Youth, families and particularly those in marginalized communities are among these statistics. A public health-focused approach is required to address and alleviate the devastating effects of gun violence. Cities and communities can no longer rely on law-enforcement strategies alone.

A robust integrated approach must include social services, community collaboration, and public health principles to interrupt, prevent, and reduce the havoc created by gun violence at the community level. There needs to be a public health emphasis on developing strategies to reduce the intensely elevated risks that the gun violence epidemic has created for youth, families, and communities.

Human decency faces continuous attacks at the primary areas of functioning, especially where cultural and multi-generational losses are commingled. Lives besieged by daily struggles and the social determinants of health can hardly be expected to move past the first level of Maslow's Hierarchy of needs, 'Safety and Security.' The WHO prescribed specific preventive measures to avert youth violence:

Preventing youth violence requires a comprehensive approach that addresses the social determinants of violence, such as income inequality, rapid demographic and social change, and low levels of social protection.

Services that identify and address the intricacies of gun-related trauma are limited. Reactionary impulses must give place to well-thought-out prevention and intervention measures that few are harnessing. The current deficit of research and policy-relevant analysis on survivors' needs and realities needs to be remedied (Buchannan, 2014, Hardiman et al., 2020).

Examining and including best practices from community agencies that have collected empirical data over years of servicing gun violence victims and survivors should be investigated and integrated as necessary. And where appropriate, synthesized material should be utilized for the greater good of youth, families, and communities.

Shootings Overview

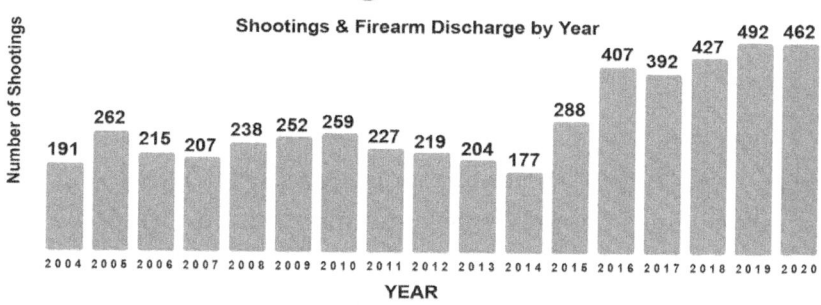

Shootings & Firearm Discharge by Year

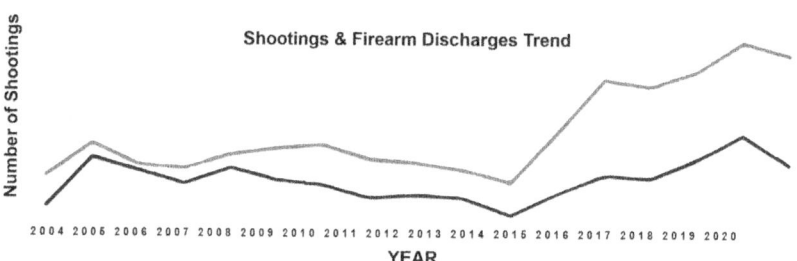

Shootings & Firearm Discharges Trend
● Incidents ● Persons Killed/Injured

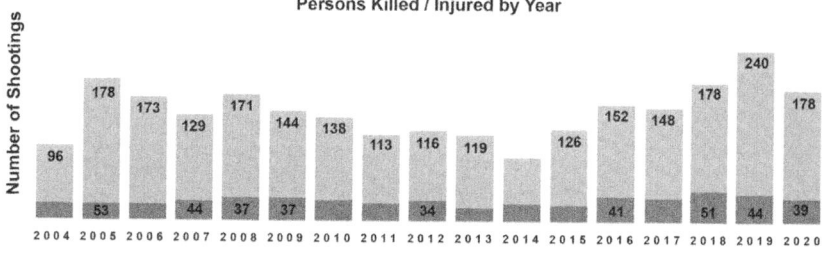

Persons Killed / Injured by Year
● Death ● Injuries

CHAPTER 2

THE GATEKEEPERS

SOCIALIZATION AND SOCIAL CHANGE BEGIN with mothers, who are considered the 'Gatekeepers' of any community. These *'Gatekeepers,'* however, are at the epicentre of gun violence trauma. They are among the most vulnerable and most affected, especially those left to carry the burden of repair and remembering. These downtrodden, deeply wounded, and often exhausted women are expected to *'soldier on.'* Not for themselves, but for other living children, for families who expect them to be *'strong,'* and for communities, where the unspoken expectation is continuity, even during, and especially in the face of, desolation.

Despite their weighed-down emotions and impoverished constitution, they epitomize Anne McCaffrey's 'Dragonsinger' as they trudge along.

Fractured Communities

> "The tears I feel today
> I'll wait to shed tomorrow.
> Though I'll not sleep this night
> Nor find surcease from sorrow.
> My eyes must keep their sight:
> I dare not be tear-blinded.
> I must be free to talk
> Not choked with grief, clear-minded.
> My mouth cannot betray
> The anguish that I know.
> Yes, I'll keep my tears 'til later:
> But my grief will never go."
> **Anne McCaffrey, Dragonsinger, 1997**

Many mothers who have lost a child or children to gun violence mask their anguish to generate a glimmer of hope and a sense of safety for their remaining children. They camouflage their emotions with false bravado most times, concealing the sheer dread of losing another child. They go through the motions of functioning, daily routines, and existing while waging an internal battle with restlessness, depression, anxiety, and suicidal thoughts. The accumulation of apprehension and stress gradually manifests through physical complaints such as recurring headaches, insomnia, depression, hypertension, irritability, hypervigilance, and other persistent ailments.

Every mother in a marginalized community lives in constant fear of their child not returning home from making a simple trip to the store. They complain of the hopelessness that threatens and often succeeds in engulfing them in immobility. Some mothers express the inability to adequately assist remaining children who are despondent, desperate, and fearful. On the social aspect, they withdraw from gatherings and becoming *grief hermits*. Friends notice their change in attitude, and behaviour, which creates a rift in relationships, and in most cases, a total cessation of friendship.

Ramifications of gun violence for mothers and families are innumerable. It is not uncommon for a vibrant, outgoing mother actively engaged in her community to rapidly become withdrawn, disinterested in life, and isolated, even within her home. Various mothers have tried to describe the emptiness they feel after a child's death. Some have likened the pain to a continuous stabbing of their heart. Others have compared it to "…a slow, vengeful death, which pervasively drains you of life, love, hope, and dreams" (Bailey, 2015), while others paint a vivid picture of being lost in a maze of repeated flashbacks, triggers, longing, and continuous anxieties (Starr, 2015).

Even mothers who have not lost a child experience the trepidation of impending gloom with the *"what ifs."* What if the police knock on their door with news they don't want to hear or see a news report like their friends experienced? Contrarily, mothers of perpetrators bear the heinousness of guilt, shame, and ostracization within their own families and community. They are openly blamed and ridiculed for the behaviour of their 'delinquent' son without anyone acknowledging that they, too, are suffering; that they too are experiencing loss, feeling isolated, ashamed, and in deep anguish.

In communities where reoccurring gun violence and impending death is a by-product of residency, many live in heightened states of continuous trauma mode. Some youth who reported abandonment from a communal and societal perspective often felt insurmountable pressures with minimal alternative against such violent recourse. The regularity of close relatives and friends' death from gun violence shrouds youth's already dismal outlook. Despite the obvious threat that they, too, could lose their lives, enduring pain justifies the overwhelming need for revenge.

Participants of intermittent focus groups shared exhaustive episodes of helplessness and loneliness, fluctuation of emotional reactions and numbness, and sensations of being/feeling boxed in.

Youth candidly disclosed that they often resorted to unwholesome repetitive outbursts of anger, revenge, and ultimately violent acts as coping strategies in hopes of alleviating anxiety, fears, and emotional pain (OOB, 2008).

Statistics Canada (2012) reiterated the plight of youth residing in marginalized neighbourhoods and their vulnerability to being victims and disabled survivors of gun violence (Janhevich, Bania, & Hastings, 2008). These youth concurrently struggle with disenfranchised grief and trauma from losing multiple friends and family members to gun violence, exposing them to lifelong experiences with psychological disablement, compounded with educational and social stagnation (Granek & Peleg-Sagy, 2015; Smith Lee, 2015).

Youth straddle between retaliation, need for healing, and fear for their lives. Amid this emotional uproar, they are also expected to function at their peak and do well in school while juggling the overwhelming challenges of natural growth and development. Those who lost siblings and friends to gun violence have difficulty functioning in school. Many suffer from depression, anxiety, insomnia, and other psychological issues, including suicidal ideologies. Truancy is common, as such prolonged health issues interfere with their concentration.

Recent research conducted by OOB with youth in Toronto who lost friends and families to gun violence affirmed that trauma experienced by these youth had the strongest correlation to violence involvement; stronger than other variables assessed such as poverty, the type of neighbourhood they live in, unemployment and education.

Trauma to gun violence exposure and loss shifts these youth's perspectives, behaviour, view of the world, and self-image. It implicates the way they grieve, their social adjustment, and pathways to their empowerment and resilience. Many also face racial and social stigma, which complicates their grieving, and hinders their healing processes.

Facilitating youth groups makes one privy to unabashed, uncensored episodes of raw emotional breakdowns. Youth between the ages of 13 and 27 and beyond welcomed their peers in a warm environment with limited adult supervision. It became commonplace to witness young men shuddering on the floor, overcome with traumatic grief. What was, and still is, most fascinating is the openness they demonstrated after such private times, emphasizing their gratitude for what they felt was lacking and identifying what was provided and the release they gained through:

a) provision of a youth-centric space and opportunity
b) the ability to feel heard and validated
c) openness to express the overwhelming need in their community for such spaces
d) encouragement to be themselves
e) support to 'cry' without judgement
f) liberty to articulate the deep emotions which propel them to violence
d) freedom to participate in the focus groups empowered them to want to be involved in community capacity building (OOB, 2008, 2010, 2012, 2015, 2017)
e) resurgence of understanding and embracing the notion of self-worth and self-care

Like the overflow of a dam, youth will eventually embrace support when their emotions become frayed from being or trying to be 'stoic.' The old, entrenched idea of masculinity includes the adage that 'men don't cry.' Yet, many youths, particularly young men, have dissipated this myth, not with a discreet tear, but with open howling, as an opportunity to release unbearable, pent-up emotions. Despite their seemingly unrealistic, immature perspectives, youth have a firm grasp of something that many cannot fathom; they have a robust belief that they have a voice and the innate power to create something from what others have incorrectly deemed as aimless.

Youth-Centric Prevention-Intervention Methods

Supporting these trauma-burdened youth requires 'youth-centric prevention/intervention' methods with stringent youth involvement during the preparation and implementation processes. Such strategies must be timely, with early prevention/intervention methods geared to their specific needs. Healing and empowerment for youth besieged by gun violence must not only include a focus on mentoring and relatable interactions, but contribution, participation, and implementation of youth opinion, to minimize and curb the long-lasting ripple effects of grief-related trauma (Weiston-Serdan, 2017).

Underlying social and economic structural problems often constitute contexts of gross inequality, marginalization, and discrimination (Duthie & Seils, 2017), which incapacitate, and in most cases, stunt the psychological progress that youth might achieve.

Emotional Intelligence (EQ), in combination with genuine capacity and interest to solve the cultural difficulty of gun violence (Gardner, 1983), has proven to be a valued instrument in combining chattels of virtues to spark and retain youth interest. Youth often mask emotions with a misguided notion that revealing their feelings demonstrates weakness. Yet, they deal with prolonged anxiety and express the hope and desire for a healthy life expectancy. With lack of concentration, truancy remains a starkly harmful by-product of the dreary trauma which plagues students.

Categorical assessment and implementation of EQ while working with youth in a setting where gun violence trauma is a factor, necessitates the inclusion of EQ's character traits to methodically steer youth towards wellness on all levels of functioning (Gardner, 1999, Goleman, 2017).

> While the foundation of combating life through gun violence is entrenched in youth day-to-day functioning, a regimented wrap-around care program can create an oasis where mentors, protégés, and respective communities can illumine crucial issues and steadily progress towards a new prototype of effective living (Weiston-Serdan, 2017).

University of Toronto Psychology Professor, Tina Malti, shared her research expertise in the first among published articles related to youth, claiming that, "Severe violence in youth is one of the most protracted social problems that cost our society much anguish, and destroys enormous social capital." She believed that in conjunction with understanding the many factors that produce youth violence, a progressive increase in successes, through prevention and intervention, could be forecasted at an early age to foresee youth who might be most at risk for violent tendencies.

Malti cited that research supports creating conditions conducive to promoting developmental pathways where empathy, perspective, purpose, and positive school and work outcomes can be enhanced to de-escalate severe violence tendencies.

Grief/Trauma and Tentacles

Over the years, victims and survivors have become creatively expressive as they often scramble to describe the whirlpool of emotions that threaten to engulf them. Many have resorted to using the graphics of nature and animals to create vivid pictures for the "grief tentacles," which creep up on them unawares. The ocean, river, rain, and the sun have all played a critical role in the dramatic narrative of gun-related trauma.

Yet, nothing is as menacing as the idea of an octopus "repeatedly zapping you, tossing you around, and dragging you into murky waters," as a few mothers have expressed. Octopuses are sea animals distinguished for their rounded bodies, bulging eyes, and long arms—all eight of them. (National Geographic, 2014). Mothers paint a gruesome picture of the flexible tentacles of this eight-legged, elongated creature, trashing them about like rag dolls during a painful upsurge where periodic episodes of retraumatization occur.

Many mothers explain that they feel the sensations as vice-grips of surging pain, making it extremely difficult for them to get out of bed, function, or even think clearly. Much like the vice-grip of heavy-duty pliers, mothers and others explain that they feel trapped for whatever time the wave of painful remembering comes over them. They liken the pain to tentacles which has the effect of suctioning and immobilizing whatever it entraps. Such is the visceral impact of a *trigger* after a traumatic loss.

Triggers are sudden, unexpected, emotional reminders of the recent death, producing waves of intensely painful feelings. Such sudden reminders cause a person to become preoccupied with the fierce feelings that overshadow everything else at that moment. Most triggers are related to the senses. Smells, hearing music, someone saying the deceased person's name, seeing a picture or favourite item, or even touching a piece of that person's clothing can be triggering.

Although trigger memory or flashbacks usually last for a few minutes, the emotions it arouses can remain for anywhere between a few minutes, a few hours and, in severe cases, a few days. It all depends on the severity of the trauma, the relationship to the lost loved one, and the temperament of the survivor. Special holidays or anniversaries can also be triggering even as people celebrate and participate in festivities.

One incident stands out as a vibrant reminder of how debilitating triggers can be. The OOB Community Interfaith Remembrance is usually held annually in December, which everyone knows is the most challenging month of the year for those who have lost a loved one. December was chosen to host the event for this specific reason: to provide a communal space where all those who have lost someone in any capacity can receive support. Although the event is open to any type of grief, we pay special tribute to mothers and grandmothers who lost someone to gun violence.

Nestled between angelic lights, this presentation tells a story. Attendees are invited to carry a picture of their lost loved ones to be exhibited and celebrated during the ceremony. In one particular year, during the event, one mother was exceptionally distraught. This particular mother's condition worsened as the ceremony progressed to where she had to be physically supported when it came time to light her loved one's memorial candle. Although it was very challenging, the gathering of community, family, and friends provided a nestling, cradling support for this mother overcome with emotions.

Christmas was an extraordinary time that she shared with her son. She explained how he delighted in the festivities and loved everything about Christmas and what it signified. Christmas planning would start on Boxing Day of one year for celebrations the following. He was overjoyed during shopping, finding unique gifts for friends and acquaintances. He was attentive and made a point of listening to what the family mentioned, surprising them with their special gift. Her voice conveyed the joy she experienced while her son was alive.

She explained how much she anticipated being at the event and what subsequently triggered her. The DJ mentioned he was dedicating a specific song to all the mothers in attendance, and that song happened to be her son's favourite. She reminisced about her son revelling in the Christmas spirit. Just like a DJ, with an imaginary microphone, he would dedicate a song, that particular song the DJ had chosen. At that moment, she envisioned her son at the last Christmas before he died while the music played, and her body and mind instantly reacted.

Later during an OOB group session, and debrief, she felt embarrassed and silly as she recalled the incident, but everyone understood and empathized with her without judgement. This incident was not only about that mother but also about the heart, compassion, and cradling within the community. Those who gathered were folks from various communities across the city. Representation was as diverse as the community itself. All types of faiths, backgrounds, and beliefs were represented there. Yet the common bond of grief was both telling and consoling, epitomizing Alphonse de Lamartine's words:

> *"Grief knit two hearts in closer bonds than happiness ever can, and common sufferings are far stronger links than common joys."*

Besides those from our group, I occasionally receive caring inquiries about that mother from folks who attended the event and remembered her story. During subsequent events, people would ask how she was doing and provide encouragement and hope. Inquiries continued over the years. Triggers, among other types of grief reactions, can have a combined effect of not only taking one back in time but of bringing one to a standstill in time.

Although these reactions lead to the crossroads of suffering, they also assist the griever in emotionally tricky situations, contributing to a positive shift forward on the journey of healing.

That mother has progressed extensively since the occurrence of that very public trigger. There were lessons to learn for everyone in attendance. Under the tutelage of grief, we all understood and identified with Victoria Alexander's quote: *"There are three needs of the griever: To find the words for the loss, to say the words aloud, and to know that the words have been heard."* In this instance, however, words were not necessary. The message was evident through the universal transmission of grief emotions.

Grief tentacles aren't restricted to those immediately related to a traumatic loss. Grief antennas also extend to others and affect those who witness the loss, hear about the trauma, or wharf their way to crisis responders such as paramedics, police officers and hospital staff, or even those hearing about a traumatic loss. People who have high levels of empathy will also be affected, as will residents within a community. Just like the dreaded octopus, trauma-tentacles reach far and wide, impacting lives and retraumatizing those who are already experiencing trauma.

Tentacles can also tug at specific areas on the grief journey where grievers find themselves immobile, unable to move ahead due to a situation that the griever might be dwelling on, such as explaining why the incident happened. Some might be stuck on seeking to reconcile the reflective processes. Our minds need to get past a thought that doesn't quite compute or doesn't sit well with our reasoning. This is when we need to debrief with a trusted friend, share with our therapist, or journal to express whatever troubling thoughts are difficult to understand fully.

Telling our story during group sessions or even allowing our creativity to flow through journaling and sharing assists in detangling our emotions. Visualizing the entrapment within grief's tentacles gives the mind permission, with the will to shift from despair to clarity, from fear to possibility, and from anguish to hope. These might be incremental steps, but there's a shift towards healing and growth each time we tell our story.

Summary

Communities are devastated by the recurring loss of young men to gun violence. Already stigmatized, marginalized, and disadvantaged, victims and survivors bear the added burden of social humiliation, reduced depletion, and psychological distress. Despite human resiliency and meaning-making, grief and loss associated with gun violence and stigmatization need to be seen as severely prolonged, traumatic experiences, requiring a tailored, prescriptive approach to the uniqueness of grieving youth and families.

Survivors of gun violence require services that extend across hospital care, mental healthcare, crisis intervention, rehabilitation, legal and other social support services (Buchanan, 2014; Oliver, 2018). As one aspect of a comprehensive program of care, grief and trauma support are needed to mitigate the physical and psychological symptoms of gun violence. Without these supports, families and communities' wellbeing is stifled, and the ability to thrive becomes non-existent.

Youth who have lost siblings and friends, and witness continuous gun violence, need to be debriefed and given appropriate opportunities to heal. Youth left without psychological support express their experience as 'wandering through mazes.' They, of course, have been taught to suppress their emotions; to continue life as usual; to deal with the continuous exposure to trauma as seemingly routine expectations. Yet, these unattended youth are expected to grow up and become model citizens.

Such neglect of their mental wellbeing and psychological betterment will only result in dysfunctional family systems, recurring violence, and lifelong frustrations. Debriefing in a safe, welcoming space for youth to explore and express their emotions must be paramount. Therefore, targeted care related to gun violence must be trauma-focused, with equal emphasis on the physical, intellectual, emotional, psycho-social, and spiritual levels.

Intentional coalition must include stakeholders' participation at the municipal, provincial, federal, and communal levels. Mutual peer support within familiar surroundings can make an important contribution to breaking cycles of violent frustrations (Buchannan, 2014) and minimize the tendency for accumulation of latent grief and PTSD (post-traumatic stress disorder).

CHAPTER 3

COMMUNITY'S MAZE

R ESIDENTS CONSTANTLY VOICE THEIR DEVASTATION related to the abrupt, sudden onset of traumatic grief. Despite ongoing anxiety that a loss could happen, families cannot mentally or emotionally prepare for the mayhem that follows the initial shock of hearing that a member was shot and killed. The onset of associated trauma to gun violence also ushers the inevitability of intermittent *retraumatization*.

Much like a maze, trauma associated with gun violence creates levels of confusing emotional pathways and tunnels that a fresh griever must go through. Sharp, hairpin turns resembling a maze indicate the triggers, flashbacks, hypervigilance, and other equally painful symptoms accompanying trauma's tentacles and ripples.

Typically, mazes have purposes that present challenges and pathways with the eventual resolve of finding one's way through to a final clearing. The intended choice is always to move forward. Once ushered into trauma's maze, the victim/survivor cannot turn back but is propelled forward to learning, growing, and ultimately healing, empowerment, and resilience.

Retraumatization is a maze widely understood as a relapse into a state of trauma triggered by the following event. It is also referred to as *"rekindled trauma,"* much like a smouldering fire is stirred to start burning brightly again. Rekindled is defined as "to rouse anew; to ignite again."

Crisis of any kind, whether man-induced, natural, or a combination, is traumatizing to anyone. For the many individuals who have already experienced it, retraumatization or rekindling that trauma is a by-product and an inevitability. Scholarly literature indicates that retraumatization is symbolic of delayed onset or reactivated symptoms related to a traumatic experience in the past (Carper et al., 2015; Kessler et al., 1999).

Even though someone might be an adult, experiencing fresh trauma reopens a previous traumatic event as far back as childhood. During peak crisis moments, many express a feeling of displacement, disruption, and even rupture of their communal and societal environments. Many find it difficult to see the world, and especially their community, as being safe. Fearful thoughts and expressions become a mantra. No one escapes the rippling ricochets of fresh trauma, which arouses secondary waves of retraumatization.

With each subsequent shooting death, those who have lost a loved one are transported back in time with disturbing, painful memories, as though they are experiencing the exact moment when they first learned of that loss. Many recall the smells, sounds, colours, time of day, and especially the surges of pain they felt. Some remember specific areas in their body where they felt a sharp, stabbing agony, only to learn that the lost loved one was shot in that area of their body.

Frequent, repetitive media reports of other shooting deaths gravely impede emotional healing and intensify retraumatization for many survivors. Research has shown that repeated exposure to graphically traumatic incidents can gravely affect and inhibit mental health, threaten the emotional health of children, and heighten acute stress for adolescents (Neria & Sullivan, 2011; Leiner et al., 2016; Busso, McLaughlin, & Sheridan, 2014).

In a society where technology and social media dominate human awareness, there is a distinct need for media exposure to provide the massive outreach that benefits the community and the everyday folks who rely on these outlets. An obvious catch-22 makes the media beneficial in disseminating, delivering and helping us attain ready information, covering events and directing where to source help. Adversely, mass media can also be detrimental to humanity's emotional wellbeing, demonstrating a propensity to display greater attention to violent events (Alexander & Klein, 2005).

Experience teaches us that communities riddled by chronic violence, particularly gun violence, relive these horrific episodes of traumatic pain with each subsequent shooting death. An assortment of emotional hysteria such as confusion, helplessness, shame, guilt, and feelings of alienation compounds the healing process. While viewing the news, one mother felt enormous empathy that moved her to instant tears as she saw the graphic detailed death of a young man who was shot multiple times. She recalled audibly voicing, *"That poor mother. Imagine getting such horrible news...."*

It was indeed horrifying for her when the dreaded knock by two police officers identified her as *"that poor mother."*

Trauma and retraumatization can both be experienced secondarily. Vicarious trauma (VT), also termed compassion fatigue, was coined by Perlman & Saakvitne (1995). It is described as the phenomenon generally associated with the "cost of caring" for others in the latest terms (Figley, 1982) and referred to as secondary traumatic stress (STS) (Stemm, 1995, 1997), and secondary victimization (SV - Figley, 1982). Many within caring professions, or facilitators who assist those with primary loss or direct trauma, often become tainted with the above conditions.

Unlike being the victim of a traumatic incident, or the primary witness of an actual trauma happening to someone else, vicarious trauma is a secondary psychological effect felt during a crisis. Secondary retraumatization and VT are indirect exposure to trauma through a firsthand recollection or a narration of the traumatic event. Spontaneous reactions to traumatic incidents warrant a gathering to decrease the surge of penetrating emotions that disturb one's natural stability.

Similar to retraumatization in its indirect association, VT can be subtle but intensely felt. It manifests through emotional symptoms, exhibiting anxiety, grief, irritability, anger, and mood swings. One may feel unsafe in surroundings, usually comfortable under normal circumstances, dissatisfaction with everyday chores, and other things such as employment or loss of one's sense of humour and joy for previously enjoyable things.

Behaviour patterns can drastically change where social enjoyments are curtailed and isolation or withdrawal from activities becomes routine. Adverse effects such as loss of appetite, insomnia, and unhealthy coping habits develop. Many resort to alcohol and, in extreme cases, participate in risky behaviour patterns and stronger substance abuse. Physical warnings such as headaches, insomnia, overtiredness, rashes, and hypervigilance are also telltale signs of VT. It's essential to pay attention to the alarm signals the body exhibits.

A universal presumption depicts trauma as pervasive in our society. It's widely believed that retraumatization, like trauma, is transferable, making trauma and vicarious trauma a part of life's daily experience. Given that trauma is experienced in both adverse events and trigger-laden words, speech and actions must be considered with the forethought of preventing harm in any capacity.

In communities where trauma and the likelihood of vicarious trauma are prevalent, attention must be placed on harm reduction and positive reinforcements that limit exposure to and prevention from violence-induced behaviours. Interactions focusing on violence-reduction in language and actions must also focus on behaviour patterns and relationships (Van der Kolk, B. 2014).

The Paradox of Connectivity and Brokenness

Understanding the cumulative impact of trauma demands that we view the correlation and paradox which surrounds that theme. Emotional or psychological trauma results from extraordinarily stressful events which shatter one's sense of security, and safety, leaving feelings of futility and powerlessness. This emotional upheaval creates an assumption that the world and surroundings are dangerous places.

Psychological trauma leaves a person struggling with upsetting emotions, memories, and anxieties that seem very present in mind, functioning, and particularly relating to others. Feelings of disconnection, numbness, and the inability to trust anyone are among the first emotions to arise. Victims and survivors withdraw from social activities, communal gatherings, friendships, and become reclusive.

Not only is the process of grieving difficult for the victim and survivor, but more so for immediate family members and close friends. It is common for close friends to feel alienated and estranged from a buddy during these very trying times. More baffling, however, is the paradoxical connection between those with a similar loss and others who share dates of losses that coincide or are in proximity.

Such connectivity makes it easier to understand Italian historian Dominici de Gravina's quote, *"It is a comfort to the unfortunate to have had companions in woe."* Traumatic hearts seem to have a language all their own when survivors naturally gravitate to each other with a level of understanding that can only be described as an innate acceptance on an ethereal level. The bond created through these other-worldly acquaintances quickly develops into a soul friendship described as *'anam cara'* by Gaelic poet O'Donohue.

Through the quiet indulgence of this soul-to-soul reaction, a healthy understanding is ignited as the art of belonging is awakened. O'Donohue described this connectivity as the fostering of a deep and special companionship. Witnessing this organic alliance produces a strong sense of hope not only to victims and survivors, but also to caregivers.

In the aftermath of traumatic deaths, hearts are understandably shattered by fresh grief, pain, and abrupt loss; minds are threadbare with unwholesome thoughts of anguish, discouragement, and fears; uncertainty penetrates futuristic plans, replacing any hint of possibility with minimal to zero prospects. An open display of two hearts and minds linking across the traumatic divide, brands Shakespeare's sharing one's misery to an admired reality. Caregivers who readily race to the beat of a traumatic drum can easily acknowledge that *"The miserable have no other medicine. But only hope..."*

The universality of trauma bridges gaps and challenges negative presumptive actions and reactions, to display an irrefutable truth: one grieving, traumatic heart identifies another. Where ethnicity and human divisiveness create lasting barriers, a heart that has experienced pain that is fresh to another, adorns the caring, compassionate soul-to-soul reality of familiarity with the road ahead.

Broken hearts are encouraged when connecting with one who has known the type of immediate pain being experienced. The expansive *'paradox of connectivity and brokenness'* binds human calamity with language cords, that only the heart can recognize during an insurmountable tragedy.

The Necessity of Wallowing

> *Friendship improves happiness and abates misery by the doubling of our joy and the dividing of our grief.*
> **- Marcus Tullius Cicero**

On the painful journey of survival and healing, frameworks of friendship accommodate the necessity to wallow through a STUG episode (Sudden ***Traumatic*** Upsurge of Grief), termed by Dr. Therese Rando in the early '90s, and adapted for this work. Although this is not a permanent situation, the onslaught of traumatic pain demands a type of 'wallowing' with which victims and survivors of fresh and latent grief become acquainted.

The 'wallowing process' is quite natural and necessary. As an intricate part of the grieving process, it teaches valuable lessons learned only from grief. During these episodes, someone in the early stages of a sudden upsurge of painful, traumatic remembering succumbs to the intensity of emotions and resolves to whatever physical reactions they feel is essential to acquire soothing. Over time, I've witnessed young and old fold themselves into fetal positions to find comfort and relief through self-soothing.

The analogy of wallowing relates to a pig rolling in mud. Traumatic grief plummets someone to dramatic reactions that might appear abnormal to others. In actuality, the person undergoing the sudden attack of pain desperately needs to yell, scream, moan, or adapt to whatever bodily form helps them cope or find reprieve from the pain. The wallowing relates to the lingering or length of time needed to bounce back from such pain. For some people, a STUG episode might last for a few minutes, while for others, it could linger for hours and, in extreme cases, days.

Cicero appropriately identifies how friendship abates misery and assists in 'dividing grief.' The fresh bond cemented between familiar losses, glides a griever through the murky waters of traumatic wallowing while the soul-friend *(anam cara)* quietly journeys alongside. No explanation is necessary; words are not needed; in fact, emotions are understood; tears, wailing, moaning, shuddering, and, yes, wallowing, are all languages of the heart during traumatic grief. Physical presence with a kind look, a touch, or even a gentle acknowledgement suffices.

Having the company of a friend who has experienced such traumatic pain is encouraging. Although they cannot take away the pain, their presence is meaningful and comforting during such testy moments. Not only does the bond deepen between such friends, but they gain better discernments into each other's emotional thresholds and develop an intensity of belonging, which speaks volumes over time.

Descriptions for these traumatic experiences differ in intensity, illustrations, and tone. Like waves, traumatic grief is relentless. The gushing water crashes ashore, recedes with the tide's ebb, but is almost immediately replaced by another high-rolling wave. Likewise, traumatic pain spools and folds like waves; it breaks and retreats recurrently, trailed by another hurtling attack.

Like a ship on the ocean, the wallowing griever is caught in a storm and needs to ride the waves until the emotions subside. Using the allegory of a captain on this traumatic ship, survivors can be gently coaxed to take small, cleansing breaths and coached on how to ride the waves. Captains in real life, understand that any effort to ride against a wave is futile and impedes progress. Although the pain can be intense, minimizing rationality, it is important to practice 'self-talk' while reminding ourselves that the painful emotions we are feeling are not permanent.

Keeping the wave imagery in mind is critical. Knowledge of an actual wave reminds us that a wave cannot remain high forever. Tides always rise and fall. So too, will any traumatic wave. It will, eventually, recede.

Over time, grievers learn that emotions come and go. Each person has a different threshold of pain tolerance, compounded by the absence of a loved one. Some are more intense than others, but the astute person gains insights during the wallowing process—each episode ushers a new learning curve, coupled with a healing shift. During these times, the most effective strategy is to allow the flow of emotions and participate in healthy ways such as breathing, crying, rocking, and moaning. Initiating and participating in wholesome activities become acquired coping skills until the crisis period ceases.

Grief is a demanding tutor that teaches the art of transformation through wallowing. Although it's always an unwanted guest, traumatic grief does its painful, quiet, yet renewing job of change in every area of our lives with personal gems of lived experience. These 'little nuggets' become priceless to our growth and understanding.

Smiles, tears, laughter, love and yes, *the dreaded* **G-word** – **'Grief,'** are all universal languages. If we're honest with ourselves, we'll openly admit that we can do without this language, that we'd rather not learn grief idioms. For those skilled at two or more languages, "grief dialect" is not one we seek to learn or add to our repertoire.

When one is new on the journey of grief, one might encounter feeling depressed, anxious, restless, unmotivated, tired, unable to sleep at times, and even distressed. **These are all normal emotions.** One should not feel alone in experiencing these emotions. All grievers will go through these reactions, whether dealing with a recent or not-so-recent loss. *What is important is how one deals with them.*

Although the natural tendency is to be alone, to keep the emotions to oneself, there are healthier ways to cope, helping the griever learn the *"universal language of grief"* and become better at identifying and managing traumatic STUGS. Over time, one can become a wise griever after learning grief's lessons and becoming more accustomed to the art of grieving.

Summary

Gun-related retraumatization has a collective impact on caregivers and the broader community, and others who view uncensored media reports of shooting deaths. A blanketed, trite warning generally precedes graphically alarming news reports, such as *"We warn you; this might be disturbing for some viewers."* Yet, like many survivors of violence, what is seen cannot be unseen, and what is experienced cannot be retracted from memory.

The imagery of indirect exposure to difficult, disturbing, and upsetting images are imprinted in memory and often weaved into one's day-to-day interactions, with reverberating effects. A strong focus must be placed on averting retraumatization, particularly vicarious trauma, for victims and survivors and the broader community, including frontline workers and other professionals.

The regularity of gun-violent deaths, retraumatization, and vicarious trauma must also become critical in addressing and providing care. Collective, prescriptive responses to trauma, in general, must be comprehensive. Holistic approaches to care should also include frontline workers who deal with siblings and families of gun violence victims daily.

Specific attention to developing trauma-informed, and violence reduction programs and strategies, must be highlighted in combatting the sinister dual forces of trauma and retraumatization. Purposeful precedence must be among the criterion which facilitates a strength-based approach to healing, empowerment, and resilience.

PART TWO

Recognition and Validation of Community Trauma

Fractured Communities

"Trauma is personal. It does not disappear if it is not validated. When it is ignored or invalidated, the silent screams continue internally, heard only by the one held captive. When someone enters the pain and hears the screams, healing can begin."
(Danielle Bernock, 2014)

EMBERS OF DEEP EMOTIONS SMOULDER within the heart of every community. Cords of love and belonging, of passionate connectivity, interlace the strong bonding fabrics which hold kin to kin; ethnicity in togetherness, and overall community within a framework of strong association.

Affinity is exceedingly important during traumatic incidents. The reoccurrence of traumatic events evokes extreme emotional reactions. Although each incident comes with devastating consequences, such a calamity draws community patrons together in an affinity that can only be described as miraculous.

Communities that experience high volumes of gun violence organically develop mutually beneficial relationships between their structures of existence. Amid other forms of daily trauma such as poverty, discrimination, oppression, and marginalization, grief-related trauma presents unique life-altering health issues that profoundly impede psychological health.

Communities are never prepared for gun violence, which is always sudden, unforeseen, and untimely. Succeeding every gun incident, whether fatal or not, victims and survivors are saddled with an assortment of mental anguish that begins a life-long journey of continuous torrent. Lives are forever altered while the cycle of violence reverberates through every inhabitant.

Recognition and validation of community trauma is an intricate part of raising awareness, not only to the issues of gun violence and its ramifications but also to the systemic issues of underserved communities.

Robert Cialdini coined *social validation*, a psychological and social phenomenon where neglect or actions termed degrading are publicly acknowledged. Although viewed as a social and psychological phenomenon, it is also known as informational social influence. For example, prime ministers have extended historic apologies, which can be seen as *'social validation.'* Today, many voices are decrying the blatant signs of invalidation for marginalized communities, particularly where the long-term effects of gun violence and trauma desecrates lives.

Social validation, or the lack thereof, is detrimental to marginalized communities that are allowed to continuously carry on with sustained discrimination, poverty, fear, anxiety, and chronic trauma. These disparagements, when experienced chronically, along with persistent incidents, such as gun violence occurrence and deaths, have cumulative negative impacts, which are fundamentally life-altering.

But in communities where gun violence trauma is 'a way of life,' other negative, cumulative, psychological distress hampers citizens' lives and livelihoods. Children especially feel that they're "less than, other than" and that their lives do not matter. Marginalized communities enduring gun violence trauma need to be acknowledged for their endurance of intense, traumatic suffering over time.

Where genuinely offered in depreciated circumstances, validation must also be supported by a well-mapped plan of action to rectify the current way of life for residents. History documents the immensely positive, progressive strides noted when citizens feel valued by word and appreciated actions. Despite the long road to healing, individual self-worth is boosted, and cultural appreciation is beginning to be highlighted as caregivers, professionals, and researchers spotlight terms such as 'cultural sensitivity' and 'cultural competence.'

Secondary, and significant benefits are two-fold when considering the immense value and sense of belonging associated with validation. Not only does acknowledgement and validation promote healing and lays the foundation for improved self-worth, but they earnestly increase the sense of belonging among patrons. Maslow's Hierarchy of needs and the Ottawa Charter emphasize the importance of *'love and belonging.'* Traumatic events are profound experiences which cause people to question their self-worth, their place in society, and in the world.

It is well established, historically, that traumatic impacts are felt weeks, months, years and even centuries later with damaging effects. The repetitive loss of lives to gun violence has become part of the fabric of existence in marginalized communities. Validation for these communities initiates acknowledging that life for youth and families is exceptionally strenuous and recognizes the immense difficulty of day-to-day functioning.

Genuine validation of violence and trauma causes the community to exhale and release emotions of dismissal to their dilemma, that encompasses years of continuous struggling. But more significantly, validating the enormous gravity of gun violence trauma unlocks the burden of feeling dismissed, overlooked, and provides a threshold for progressive healing and restoration.

Acknowledgement of the insurmountable anguish resulting from injuries and traumatic deaths from gun violence, must be encouraged and voiced for the grave detriments to the health and well-being of all community members. Each incident must be validated with the intensity of the overall torrents of anguish, where poverty intersects with a need for survival; where fear of being killed makes some resort to owning a gun; and where protecting one's life immediately indicates violence.

Youth already have the arduous task of maneuvering the strenuous demands of natural growth and development in adolescence. Decision-making, growth spurts, and hormonal changes are daily stressors that complicate their lives. Gun violence trauma compounds the situation for many youths, and presents an unwholesome number of successive issues that not only threaten, but extinguish their lives.

Though natural for expectant growth and development, the psychological distress of body image often poses a self-conscious image for youth who might be struggling to fit in with their peers. Body shape and characteristics consume their perceptions making this period a perplexing time for most young people.

During adolescence, youth gravitate to and rely heavily on peer opinion. They relate to and readily confide in their friends. It is not unusual for youth to distance themselves from parental guidance or advice. Many feel they have little in common with those in leadership positions, whether parents, teachers, or other professionals.

These are normal reactions during puberty, as youth seek to determine sexual orientation, career paths, and different functional beliefs. Arguments with parents are more frequent as they strive to gain independence. Although there are constant struggles between adolescents and parents, youth know that parents are critical to the family dynamics and are their strongest support system.

Studies and research specify that trauma overloads the brain, limits its ability to problem-solve, taking away the ability to cope (Porges et al., (2020). Dealing with trauma during these critical times further infuriates an already annoying situation for youth. Those who lose a sibling or close friend face exorbitant anguish, which is often left untreated. During these critical times, patience and gentle reassurances with kind persistence remind youth that the support offered is genuine and will not be withdrawn.

Youth have developed a misconstrued perception that adult support usually comes with conformity. With consistent demonstration of sincere concern for their wellbeing, these feelings eventually dissipate. Cautiousness is generally a humanistic behaviour, especially in the early stages of trauma. This instinctive approach is understandable. When we have experienced continuous disillusionment, a natural human response is to protect one's emotions. Youth are not dissimilar in assuming this attitude.

Most youth I've worked with are relatively guarded in the early stages of trauma interactions, until they gradually warm up to the consistent show of concern, and the honest approach over time. Such behaviour must not be seen as insolent, but rather understood within the context of the circumstances, especially if it relates to fresh trauma. The situation must also be viewed through the lens of community context, with a keen eye on recurring incidents.

While young people's response to gun violence might be readily predicted within the scope of natural growth and development, children, on the other hand, pose different issues. Treatment for, and support extended to children from infancy to pre-teen, must be straddled and age-appropriate.

Children who once played freely will develop episodes of longing and yearning when they lose a family member. Their childhood days have been abruptly and negatively interrupted. Nightmares, bed-wetting, fears, anxieties, and insecurities become lingering side-effects. Many become sullen, withdrawn, disinterested in socializing and whiny. In extreme cases, some become clingy or have difficulty sleeping. They might participate in self-harm, including verbal and physical lashing out.

Gun-related trauma causes children to mistrust adults and those who are supposed to protect them, fearing abandonment. Their outlook on home, community, and the world is significantly altered after experiencing gun-related trauma.

Adverse events from childhood mould minds, and create unwholesome perceptions of relationships and the world. Children often have difficulty identifying, expressing, and dealing with complex trauma like gun violence, with their limited vocabulary. Simple, age-appropriate explanations with genuine concerns must be emphasized. Consequently, a young mind would intercept where a harmful experience becomes too challenging to manage, and painful memories will lay dormant in a child's mind to resurface in adolescence or adulthood.

Retention of such graphically painful experiences typically manifests through depression, anxiety, rapid mood swings, angry outbursts, and hitting. Patience, understanding, and kindness need to be exercised.

CHAPTER 4

GRIEF-RELATED TRAUMA

Perpetrators and Associates

MARGINALIZATION BY THOSE ALREADY MARGINALIZED is a compounding factor during a gun violence death. Regrettably, this occurrence is real and negatively contributes to an already polarized situation. Mothers and families of the perpetrator of a gun violence death, face excruciating ostracization within their community.

These members are blatantly shunned from gatherings; they are excluded from internal information; they are blamed, insulted, and ridiculed. In extreme cases, any attempts on their part to express condolences are openly rejected. In worst scenarios, they are overtly denied any opportunity to attend vigils, wakes, or funerals.

Within the complexity of these situations, emotions are not only intensely heightened but irrational and clouded. Freshly traumatized families are at an amplified level of concentrated trauma. Reason and objectivity cannot even be imagined or expected. The sudden death of their son and, in rare cases, their daughter consumes these families. Even when the perpetrator's family member was a close friend, well-known, or even familiar with the family, nothing alters these organically painful responses.

One antagonizing incident created such turmoil that it became the catalyst which propelled me to gaze with intently candid eyes at grief, loss, and trauma, from a perpetrator's vantage point.

One mother was feeling so tremendously distraught at the news that her son pulled the trigger, resulting in a young man's demise, that she reached out to the mother of that lost youth. With instinctive empathy, she put herself in that mother's place, envisioning how she would feel if that were one of her sons. She was harshly reprimanded and advised never to call again. Despite such severe treatments, the guilt, shame, and sorrow she felt pushed her to try again. She attended a vigil but was escorted out of the space, with others joining in the ridicule. That insulted mother made a final attempt at expressing her sympathy by attending the funeral but was again forcibly removed with, *"You should be ashamed to show your face here."*

Although denigrated with the title of "perpetrator mom," this mother has suffered a profound loss and is also experiencing fresh trauma. Not only was her son arrested and convicted of a deadly crime, but she endured several accumulated losses.

She lost her relationship with her son, which was definitely altered; she lost seeing her son every day; she lost attending his graduation and the hopes and dreams for her son's future. Communally, she lost her identity as a welcomed resident. She lost love and belonging, friends, associates, group attendance,

Grief-Related Trauma

and inclusivity. The ebb and flow of the 'tide of guilt' that she carried with her incessantly in the early years will keep ebbing and flowing all her life.

Doing justice to such an unfortunate predicament necessitated a thorough exploration of how a committer's mother and family would feel in that dilemma. Despite this unfortunate plight, these families and associates need to be supported, validated, and encouraged to heal. Any traumatic situation includes authentic delving into the Psychological First Aid and eCPR (Emotional CPR), which is desperately needed during trauma.

That mother, too, needs to be supported, affirmed, and accompanied on the journey towards healing and restoration. The dubbed name *"mother of the perpetrator"* will be continuously mentioned whenever she is addressed. Even if/when it is not audibly stated, subtle indicators and gestures will not be missed or mistaken. Whispers, attitudes, behaviours, looks and body language will make inferences. She will be openly snubbed and dismissed. Many will choose to look past or walk past her without acknowledgement. That insinuation will always be present in her mind.

It takes progressive, compassionate people who can objectively view the situation through a suffering mothers' eyes to support a mother whose son took another's life. These individuals must be impartial across the spectrum. Specific criteria of neutrality are the primary characteristic, followed by compassion and a willingness to work alongside grieving, traumatized women.

Given the situation's complexities, I worked with volunteers and already trained facilitators who demonstrated neutral compassion, despite the situation. These volunteers had to display distinctive signs of objectivity in attitude, viewpoint, and intent. Some had accompanied me on initial crisis response, where I observed their demeanour, tone of voice, facial expressions, and body language. Intensive training followed the screening process, where the concentration was understanding the trauma that relatives of a perpetrator experiences and identifying the issues they faced.

Comforting someone during grief is a delicate art, where understanding sets the stage for empathy to flourish. During fresh trauma, a well-watered bed of consideration can be made, where a caring person can listen attentively with the ears, the body, and the senses, while being present in the moment. Traumatic individuals have a heightened awareness that makes them acutely conscious of not only what's said but how it's extended. Applying best traumatic practices during these tense periods abates strife and significantly lessens the already heavy affliction accompanying gun violence.

Although the healing process can be strenuous, tensions do lessen over time, and concessions are made where insensitivity gives way to understanding that, in most cases, mothers are not responsible for their children's actions. Over time, some mothers opt to relocate, whereas others gradually acquire healing and ample empowerment to rise above the tumultuous waves to steady, progressive resilience. They affirm that the traumatic ache diminishes but is always one trigger away.

Providing competent, empathetic care to these particular cases requires a mindset where those affected are not harshly judged, but accompanied with the sensitivity that comes from putting oneself in another's shoes and remembering the adage *"There but for the grace of God, go I."* (Bradford, 1843).

Legacies of Trauma

Gun violence inflicts a trauma that remains a lifetime scourge. The effects of this stealthy type of trauma are lingering and debilitating, paralleling the indelible monument of a *'living legacy.'*

My continuing work with survivors acknowledges this emerging field of study's significance and ratifies an earnest inquiry into the serious difficulties it presents for trauma survivors.

Following the death of a child and the subsequent tedious tasks of choosing clothes for the burial, every mother I worked with over the years repeat the woeful mantra; *I don't want my child's death to be in vain.* Interest in *the legacy of trauma* is becoming prevalent, much like intergenerational trauma has been highlighted. Although this area is rarely raised or discussed, it warrants exploration within the context of generations of traumatic experiences.

Maria Yellow Horse Brave Heart-Jordan used research conducted on Holocaust survivors in the 1980s to convey "the collective and compounding emotional and psychological injury over the lifespan that is multigenerational." Brave Heart-Jordan identified comparable clusters of events to show intergenerational trauma across generations. The legacy of trauma correlates with the meaning-making legacies, diminishing the hopelessness surrounding a youth's death to gun violence.

Symbolically, death anniversaries keep the memory of a lost loved one alive. This significant ritual assists those who actively engage in the process to willfully remember, participate in some commemorative ceremony, and travel through the painful memory chambers of the gruelling onset of trauma. These occasions, though necessary, are also bittersweet with haunting pain.

Despite the satisfaction of meaning-making through efforts to keep the lost child's memory alive during expressive events, the convoluted contrast of the legacy of trauma is also resurfaced. The legacy of trauma is imposed and re-experienced through each retelling of a trauma story.

Mothers relive these piercingly painful periods while sharing their stories through freshly open wounds of scar-tissue sentiments. Unresolved emotions such as grief, anger, blame, shame, and especially guilt linger after these events, creating secondary issues. Additionally, it is vitally important that the *'re-opening traumatic wound syndrome'* be explored. During any commemoration, it is customary for trauma survivors to time travel back to the initial incident, where sounds, smells, imagery, and expressed words are freshly re-experienced.

Survivors must be encouraged and assisted in exploring these repetitive emotions, much like a debriefing session, to minimize the level of legacy pain they're experiencing.

After such events, debriefing offered to survivors of traumatic situations allows them to identify fresh, familiar, and latent emotions. Participation in this "self-examination" enables them to practice active coping, pinpoint what they need, and assists them in shifting to a new level of understanding and healing. Where debriefing does not occur, survivors can remain in this altered space of *'legacy pain,'* which can cause regression on their healing journey.

Multi-generational households also experience the legacy of trauma. Although the levels of trauma are in varying stages and effects, this cumulative type of emotional pain has a crippling impact on families and homes. It can be seen through current generations as festering gaps where grandparents, parents, siblings, and extended families are each affected in specific ways depending on their temperament, length of time since the loss, and of course, their relationship with the lost relative.

Regrettably, for these households, the influence of resurging legacy trauma lingers in stages as the uniqueness of grieving is for everyone. Emerging interests and information from such self-examination will undoubtedly produce valuable insight into regulating responses for legacy trauma. Vigilance with customized approaches provides better insight into survivors' needs and the importance of tailored, supportive responses to inform positive reactions.

In conjunction with client participation, changes in systemic approaches further enhance members' contribution within multi-generational households, to access and combine their inherent capacity to process these intruding emotions adequately. With consistent attention to, and processing of the complexities of legacy trauma, families can process pre-existing emotions, apply practical strategies to identify and address their pain, and eventually attain healing towards empowerment.

Summary

> *"But almost always, during the initial stage of the struggle, the oppressed, instead of striving for liberation, tend themselves to become oppressors, or "sub-oppressors."*
> - **Paulo Freire, Pedagogy of the Oppressed**

Boundaries are non-existent in gun violence trauma. With super-imposed traumatic tentacles, it straddles across age, race, gender, status, ethnicity, and socioeconomic status. In recent years sexual orientation has been accosted as women and young girls fall prey to blurry margins. These disastrous complexities manifest at higher levels of intensity in densely populated communities, where poverty, marginalization, and racial and structural disparities contribute to the daily experiences for many.

Repetitive violence becomes a way of life; scarcity, hunger and food insecurity are entrenched in the weaving of everyday language; youth desperation merges with distress, anxiety, and eventual harmful activities; empathy is slowly replaced with desensitization; the endurance of psychological trauma is misconstrued within the actions of shunning, blaming, and internal oppression.

Scholars have flagged these unresolved, lingering trauma associations with racial and ethnic populations, decrying the sufferings of significant intergenerational losses and assaults on their culture and wellbeing (Dass-Brailsford, 2007; O'Neil, 2017). Ethnicity and cultural dissonance, which usually backdrops to surfacing issues, must be observed within a framework where committed intent is implemented to identify, curb, and promote healing for gun violence trauma.

Accumulated disenfranchisements heaped on families and communities, for centuries, necessitates recognition and validation, with deliberate, practical solutions that will minimize traumatic pain and promote healing.

CHAPTER 5

NEEDS ASSESSMENT

"The amount of respect any idea deserves is revealed by the verifiable facts it contains."
- **C.A.A. Savastano, Goodreads**

FOLLOWING THE FATAL SHOOTING OF a 15-year-old, media dubbed 2005 as 'the Year of the Gun' in Toronto. The startling revelation of gun violence trauma was further heightened with another fatality at a high school, reverberating through the years to the present, in shocking numbers. Despite a flurry of talks to curtail gun violence, Toronto, and Canada, have been reactionary both in response to gun violence deaths and prevention/intervention measures for survivors. We have regressed significantly with efforts to contain or minimize gun violence and the trauma associated with it.

Notwithstanding the continuous gun violence fatalities, needs assessments are requested to legitimize gun-related trauma.

My first needs assessment in 2006, focused mainly on high school youth and parents, revealed an astounding high velocity of the ripple effects associated with gun violence. Our findings were corroborated by the extensive literature review and public consultations from the Roots of Violence Youth Violence Report (McMurtry & Curling 2008), conducted with community input across Ontario. Recommendations pinpointed specific attention be placed on "adopting a more coordinated, more comprehensive, and more community-focused approach to reduce youth violence."

Even back then, racism was flagged among the very serious problems encountered in neighbourhoods, characterized by the severe, concentrated, and growing disadvantages that were being unaddressed. Thirteen years later, these highlighted issues continue to pose detriments to the city's and provinces' social fabric. The report further identified the critical juncture of Ontario "being at an important crossroad" incubating an increase in youth violence.

> The growth in the prevalence of both guns and gangs, neighbourhoods trapped in a downward cycle of disadvantage and being challenged to provide the solidarity and positive role-modelling needed to help stem the violence, and a broader community inclined to write off these youth and these communities because they see them as the source of this problem rather than its victims (McMurtry & Curling 2008).

Periodic needs assessments continue to highlight the gravity and the tumbling spiral of health-promotion, in contrast to the accelerated intensification in youth deaths.

One would be hard-pressed to find a child or youth in any marginalized community, who has not been inadvertently affected by gun violence trauma. Many have lost siblings, friends, acquaintances, or even themselves been shot. In most cases, psychological and physical scars are among the everyday baggage they carry. With these permanent burdens, communities also face constant retraumatization from frequent and continuous gun violence and deaths.

Gathering, analyzing, and synthesizing information to endorse positive change are beneficial efforts to promote favourable evolution. Needs assessment is only effective if it offers concrete evidence to determine which solution is best for achieving the desired results and, further, implementing them.

After 17 years of educating, supporting, and advocating for gun violence victims and survivors, the implementation of the Roots of Violence Report is yet to be established.

Necessary Time and Space

There are designated communal spaces that are termed 'necessary,' especially during a crisis. Human beings instinctively gravitate to these necessary spaces immediately following a shooting death. Random areas such as apartment buildings, street corners, alleyways, parks and regrettably, homes are among those spaces. Community centres often become the gravitating spaces, except if the family has no objections to folks being at their homes. Make-shift memorials are routinely erected, even in alleyways, to recognize a lost life.

Space takes on various roles of the gathering area, containing emotions and dividing fresh grief. It is critical that wherever that communal space is established, everyone shows respect and empathy to those who are freshly grieving.

Yet, no matter how often a shooting death occurs, a community is never prepared. Not really. As an in-house therapist at OOB, I created and continue to teach a 10-session, intensive and comprehensive trauma-focused training for volunteers and facilitators. We cover theoretical material where volunteers are educated in understanding grief, loss, and trauma. Knowing what grief is and how it affects others, including the facilitator, is critical to providing competent support.

Such familiarity helps to minimize the initial shock of arriving at a scene and gets one better prepared to assist and gather data. We rehearse the 'dos and don'ts' of the initial response to a location or the home of a fresh shooting.

Volunteers must go through these rigorous training sessions to better equip themselves on three levels: first, to gain ample knowledge of trauma; second, to identify and manage personal triggers; and third, to access competency to support others adequately. Volunteers are reminded of the significance of removing themselves from the area if they cannot compose themselves sufficiently to assist the immediate family and others effectively.

Feeling and being weepy is humane, but not if the affected parties become the ones doing the comforting. These sessions are offered at the introductory level and are mandatory for all OOB volunteers. The intermediary level is for anyone who wants to respond to a crisis, and the advanced level is for those interested in facilitating groups for victims and survivors.

Classified as an underserved community, Jane and Finch inexplicably experiences the highest volume of shooting activities and deaths in Toronto, Canada. Similarly, our community also ranks high on the social, economic, and racial inequities scale. Issues of racism, profiling, discriminatory policies, exclusion, and numerous incarcerations are among the many overbearing factors which compound and contribute to gun violence and trauma.

When a youth death occurs, residents bond together in a unique understanding that exemplifies our caring, sensitive community. Again, the adage is foremost in the minds of empathizers: *"There, but for the grace of God, go I."*

Holding Space

> *"Oh, the comfort, the inexpressible comfort of feeling safe with a person; having neither to weigh thoughts nor measure words, but to pour them all out, just as they are, chaff and grain together, knowing that a faithful hand will take and sift them, keep what is worth keeping, and then, with a breath of kindness, blow the rest away."*
> **- Dinah Maria Mulock Craik, A Life For A Life**

Empathy is quite different from kindness. It's an emotion that allows us to put ourselves in another person's place and get a better sense of what they are feeling at any given moment. It's a healthy way to show care and concern for another person. Empathy is apparent during fresh or latent grief and is offered without hesitation. Over time, I've discovered that we all have different levels of empathy, to which some scientists agree. People in helping professions have rich supplies of kindness and face potential burnout if ample, holistic self-care isn't practiced.

Although empathy is genetically inherent, scientists report that folks with limited or no empathy can cultivate this highly recognized and desirable trait. (Zaki, 2019, 2020). Zaki provides intriguing stories while arguing this stance, using research to verify that empathy can be developed, acquired, and enhanced over time.

Demonstrating genuine empathy is an art that is unabashed during fresh grief and trauma. Human hearts can identify and, better yet, feel and receive empathy. Mothers have recounted how warm they felt after receiving a genuine, empathetic hug from someone during their darkest moments of trauma. Much like the art of comforting, although some people are more empathetic than others, we are all capable of showing care and concern for ourselves, others, and our community.

'Holding space' is the concept of physically being with someone at their lowest grieving period, and on a holistic level, providing the emotional, mental, psychological, and even spiritual support they need. While some people are uncomfortable with silence, during holding space, a person can allow silence to slide by without hastening to say anything, especially to reserve judgment.

Hurting hearts are highly charged and super sensitive. These hearts can identify empathy which creates fertile *'space'* where "friendship improves happiness and abates misery, by the doubling of joy…and the dividing of…grief." An empathetic presence works wonders for any grieving heart. Often, without uttering a word, a gentle caring touch allows one's presence to keep the space and provide solace for another.

It is becoming an imaginary 'container' for the overwhelming emotions that are surfacing. Like an actual container, secure in its ability to *'hold-in-place,'* we need to be centred and grounded while holding space to be effective supporters. The steadiness exhibited provides the temporary support necessary for our friend or companion to lean on. Our presence offers a strong sense of security so that person's emotions can flow unhindered through the secure environment.

Inner and outer virtues play an equally critical role during this emotional toggle-sharing. The *'holder'* needs to be in a state of humility with a conscientious consideration of the other person, whose emotions require that holder to allow the other's emotions to flow unhindered. It is also crucial to remember that this essential holding pattern is not about the holder, but the person in crisis. Holding space is an incredibly unselfish gift we provide to a loved one or friend during a low point, when their container is overflowing with raw, traumatic emotions.

The concept of holding space originated with Heather Plett after experiencing multiple losses. Exceptional art, music and poetry have been created with grief, loss, and trauma as relentless instigators, especially after experiencing support while holding space. Grief's tutoring heightens awareness and helps us shift from pain to transformation, and in many cases, to creative genius.

Freshman Griever

Grief's universality accommodates and entertains idioms, metaphors, and allegories from around the globe. Despite the apparent understanding it generates, using the expression that someone is experiencing fresh grief has become well-known and overused.

During my final year at seminary, I aspired to find a new word, a different expression for this well-accepted phrase. My mind sifted through the already familiar grief-related vocabulary until it meditated on the freshmen coming in for the new semester. Instinctively, the eyes, mind, and revelation raised consciousness with the 'ah-ha moment.' Webster's definition deemed a 'freshman' as "A first year, or frosh—a person in the first year at an educational institution, usually a secondary or post-secondary school." It was simple enough for any age to grasp.

For this book's purpose, someone experiencing their first traumatic grief is a *"Freshman- griever."* The beginning of loss initiates grievers to the tunnel of 'firsts' without their loved ones. Once ushered past the entrance, the journey begins with no recourse but to move forward. First birthday, first anniversary, first family gathering, holidays and other special days specific to various families. For relatives whose kids are still in high school or university, graduations and weddings create despondency without that special someone to participate in the celebrations.

Uniqueness allows each person to meander through the maze of grief at their own pace and in their distinctive way. What might seem natural and easy to sift through for some is not the same for others. The level of agonizing intensity depends on the closeness of that specific relationship, while the journey's length would vary both in time and velocity. The struggle of mourning and variations of coping are also different. However, grief's painful process is the one characteristic that is common for everyone on the journey to adjustment and healing.

We must also be aware that grief is not a linear but a deviating process. Confusion will cloud judgements, and emotions will fluctuate without warning. Some days will start on an even keel only to plummet without warning. For some people, appetite will dwindle, while for others, food will seem to be comforting. Body aches will develop where there were no problems before, and insomnia inevitably becomes a constant companion for long nights of restlessness and yearnings.

There are some vital factors with identifiable situations to avoid. Self-care must be a priority—adequate rest and sleep help to renew one's nerve synapses. Synapses are essential to the transmission of nervous impulses, which assist in minute details of functioning. Grief, especially if it's sudden, is much like a total body shock wave. This type of shock affects the emotional, mental, intellectual, physical, psycho-social, and spiritual levels of functioning. Short-term memory becomes a constant companion but will gradually improve. Rest and sleep rejuvenate the brain and sharpens the nerves.

Concurrently, the opposite might occur where folks would not want to get out of bed. Some would need coaxing and sometimes firm insistence to get up and move around or engage in minute duties. Where appetite is affected, effort must be taken to have smaller meals or drinks to keep hydrated.

People generally neglect body care when depression seeps in. This is a critical time for relatives and friends to show concern, encourage and assist where necessary. Having a shower or bath revitalizes the body and stimulates the mood. Going for a short walk is also invigorating.

Single mothers, in comparison, neglect themselves as they focus on remaining children. *Fresh-man* survivor moms need extra TLC (tender, loving, care) integrated with reminders. Consistent support needs to be provided to these 'trooper survivors.' During the early days, weeks, months after the funeral, they need to be supported, checked on regularly, and encouraged through the compacted struggle that follows.

After the bustle of activities has subsided and quietness sets in, exhaustion, overwhelming anxiety, and deep depression usually manifest. Regular check-ins are compulsory during this highly critical time for these moms, who are expected to soldier on, despite their feelings of insurmountable pain and loss.

The most important thing to highlight is the need to refrain from making any major decisions during the first year of 'freshman grieving.' Thoughts are unbalanced, perceptions and ideas are very unstable. These areas of concern might seem insignificant, but to a "Freshman griever," they exemplify the difference between suppressed grief and the ability to heal at a steady pace.

Summary

The scarcity of resources and erratic community-based grief support to meet survivors' complex and long-term trauma needs prolong the grief journey and negatively obstructs the healing process. Implementation of consistent trauma-focused strategies must be enacted to replace the frugal, reactionary responses with reliable therapeutic strategies to:

a) provide a safe space of belonging to relieve survivors' emotional and psychological pain.
b) offer reliable coping strategies to relieve fresh and latent grief with layered retraumatization.
c) improve social interactions to enhance survivors' coping capacity.

Although we boast that Canada has stricter gun laws than the US, the disheartening rate of gun-related deaths continues to plague families and communities across our country, and particularly in Toronto. Families are inundated with the frequency of gun-related deaths and the engorged retraumatization that follows.

A unified strategy of prevention and intervention measures with trauma-focused education and sustainable post-traumatic care is the singular approach to address this gun violence pandemic.

Repetitive traumatic events are known to have detrimental long-term impacts on both mental and physical health. With gun violence, cumulative trauma is the recurrent incidents, frequent deaths and retraumatization that communities continuously endure. Planned, customized responses that focus on cultural dissonance, must be established to provide needed reprieve from this deadly stressor, and to regulate the systemic issues perpetuating these cycles.

CHAPTER 6

GETTING A GRIP ON GRIEF

During the early stages of traumatic loss, mothers and their families experiencing gun-violence survivorship trauma, require services beyond existing mental health care and rehabilitation (Buchanan, 2014).

A myriad of complexities is embedded within the webbed cycles of grief, loss, and trauma. Self-isolation has become a noticeably common phenomenon, particularly in the early stages of fresh grief. During group sessions, mothers, and primarily "Freshman grievers," expressed the need for ruminating without the chatter they had been experiencing. Voices, though respectful, engaged in varying degrees of low-toned conversations; demanding duties and expectations in preparation for a vigil, funeral, burial and the dreaded 'post-gathering.'

On the downturn, tasks of signing/obtaining official documents, ratifying the customary thank-you notes, including the at-home stressors, are consistently rearing their heads. The need to self-isolate covertly creeps in, with small refusals initially, progressing steadily to full-blown withdrawal from household activities. Removal might not be to the customary spaces of bedrooms or houses but can also be done overtly through silent presence and non-participation.

One mother disclosed that she withdrew to the cemetery, where she spent countless hours isolated from the outside world. When at home, her room became her ideal sanctuary. This mother divulged how she revelled in the curtailed interruptions as she ruminated on various memories of her son. While pondering on happy times is categorized as healthy grieving and is readily encouraged, lengthy isolation presents one of the ominous "red flags" in grief, which signifies potential threat.

As in childhood, grievers need to take baby steps in the process of becoming accustomed to, and accepting the yearning, longing, and absence of the lost loved one. Grieving is a steady, propelling process in an unfamiliar terrain, where lessons in healing are mandatory, and growth is imminent. Entrance to the process equates to standing at the threshold of a tunnel without the option of turning back. Once the grief process has begun, we might linger at the entrance or even sit midway, but sorrow's task urges us forward to the opposite end of the tunnel.

Getting a grip on grief allegorizes the process of acceptance that every griever must realize, even if we don't understand it, and especially when we would rather not be on its territory.

Grief's uniqueness specifies each person's solitary path through sorrow's tunnel. Among the many lessons to be learned, another alarming contradiction also shrouds the grieving concept. Grief is inherently a solo journey. One might encounter friends who become buddies or helpers, advisors and associates who contribute to their progress, but the journey of learning and growth is respectively a private one. It begins with this distinct understanding.

Although one desires time to stand still, life continues, and grief's lesson will forever be nudging one forward.

Distinctive from acceptance, this critical level of initial understanding provides a handle that changes the mindset and allows the psyche to begin the grieving process. Symbolically, grasping this concept, though painful, makes a massive difference in how one heals from trauma and how meandering the journey would ultimately become. The lengthy journey to healing will not be direct. Twisting, co-jostling, and spiralling will become familiar experiences; days will seem longer than others; repetitive cycles of behaviours will become mundane, while grief, loss and trauma instructions demand better understanding.

No two people grieve the same. Scholars outline stages of grief that are much like an indulgence and, admitting that, much as we might love to, we cannot turn back time. As a tutor, this is the first lesson in acceptance which must be grasped at the entrance of the grief/trauma tunnel.

In marginalized communities where huge gaps remain for community-based grief and trauma support, to meet survivors' complex and long-term trauma needs, residents undergo incessant post-traumatic effects from gun violence. Children, youth, families, and communities are left with unaddressed post-care, where debilitating psycho-social challenges continue to frame their jagged healing path, as they struggle to move forward.

Psychological Upheaval

"The conflict between the will to deny horrible events and the will to proclaim them aloud is the central dialectic of psychological trauma."
– Judith Lewis Herman

Psychological trauma affects us on all levels of human functioning. Emotional responses at the onset of receiving traumatic news, vary from person to person. Due to the intensity of trauma associated with gun violence, and the lifelong, enduring after-effects it infuses, this chapter highlights some of the explosive emotional rollercoaster turmoil, which occurs both internally and externally. The intensity will be different for everyone, with the uniqueness of grief and trauma.

No one can anticipate how someone might react to upsetting news unless and until it happens.

Emotions that surface during these strenuous times are to be acknowledged without judgement. Feelings are our body's response to whatever is happening around us and are neither good nor bad. When we name those feelings, our bodies understand that the signals being sent are registered. We are in tune with what's happening, even if our body succumbs to the bombardment of successive emotions being itemized.

The first mother who fainted after hearing that her son was killed didn't faint until *after* I spoke with her for about 45 minutes. Her voice was monotone as she softly responded during our conversation. She declined my suggestion to sit and felt the need to pace. Her mind was trying to process the news while at the same time thinking that the police had mistaken her son's identity for someone else's.

Understanding the abruptness of reactions, I paced with and stayed close to her. I kept a close eye on this mother and finally insisted that she sit as I noticed her eyes moving quickly back and forth. As her body touched the couch, she flopped and fainted. After she regained consciousness, the first torrent of weeping initiated her traumatic grief journey.

Gun Violence Education & Grief/Trauma Education

> *"When someone dies instantly, then I think the well of grief and disbelief all mixed in with it is unfathomable. And when murder is involved, that just takes it into a whole new place. There is an extra dimension you just can't compute or deal with."*
> **- Andrew Buchan**

Predictable, customary emotional responses to sad, traumatic news are shock, denial, numbness, disbelief, and helplessness. For those whose constitutions are strong, fainting might not be included in the automatic body reactions which typically follow. Although the human body is strong enough to survive and withstand many shock waves, dealing with the suddenness of traumatic news might generate other reactions that must be monitored.

To adjust and create self-protection, our senses participate with the body as a combined unit to assist in managing the extra stimulus we're receiving. Each person will respond differently, but it's important to understand that there are times when we will need assistance.

Learning of a sudden, traumatic death ranks high on the Richter scale of inflated sad news. These physical, emotional, and other reactions are among the many mothers, families, and communities have attested to, some of which I have witnessed first-hand.

Some people experience profuse sweating, nausea and vomiting, diarrhea, or other symptoms. Jittery feelings, tremors and wobbly legs might also manifest, but these reactions are compensating and will eventually fade as quickly as they appear. We might not be at our peak health mentally, but we can trust that our bodies will do whatever is necessary to help us cope, even it means making frequent trips to the washroom.

Our job during those times is to be gentle with ourselves. Sit, rest if/when sensations of faintness arise and keep hydrated. Loss of appetite might be a symptom but keep drinking fluids, tea, or soup to keep thoughts clear and focused. Allow others to assist and support when self-care becomes challenging, especially if there are dependent survivors. Self-compassion might be a new trait to learn for anyone who is usually active. Where one is used to extending care and compassion to others, there must be the grace to accept care for oneself. The urgent need is to be gentle with oneself.

Putting Emotions in Perspective

> *"Feelings are something you have; not something you are."*
> **– Shannon L. Alder**

It is difficult to reconcile the enormous doubt and denial related to unexpected death. Human tendency is the overwhelming urge to ignore the awful news and rationalize that there's been a huge mistake. These feelings are jostled with an intense yearning and longing to touch or hug the person to authenticate the false premise that the news is untrue.

Mothers hunt for words to explain and express the conflicting feelings of confusion that irritate them. One mother recalled how she desperately needed to see her son's body and the agony she endured while waiting for two weeks. As part of the ongoing investigation, the coroner must do an autopsy. This mother felt afraid to even mention how muddled her thoughts were. She was convinced that she heard her son's voice calling her name, which he usually did, and followed his hurried footsteps coming through the door. This is one of the earliest cases I encountered of "bereavement hallucination."

Bereavement hallucination is "sensing the presence of a deceased loved one." Although spoken of as "a commonly reported phenomenon," the earliest reference is a 2002 report by German researchers on a middle-aged woman grieving her daughter's death. After reviewing reported cases, the DSM-5 concluded that these incidents could be termed as *"Persistent complex bereavement disorder."*

Well-known singer, Celine Dion, shocked the world by revealing that she senses her husband's presence, talks to him at times, and even hears his voice a year after his death. Her disclosure was met with a range of convoluted reactions, but researchers continue to substantiate this disquieting phenomenon. During our post-care sessions, many mothers and other grievers have disclosed hearing their loved one's voice, sensing their presence and even 'catching a whiff of their cologne.'

Bereavement Hallucination further complicates traumatic situations and the grieving process. Therefore, it is essential to initiate self-care from the onset of trauma and introduce an *"Accountability Partner"* who will consistently work with those affected by trauma. The Accountability Partner is usually another mother who has completed our 10-week training session, is sufficiently comfortable with her own grief, and has healed sufficiently to assist a Freshman griever.

Accepting help for self-care during the first week of learning about a sudden death is an excellent first step in self-care. Maybe just allowing someone to run a bath or assist with hair care might be simple areas to start. Practicing self-care might be foreign for those of us who like to do things ourselves, but please consider the circumstances and accept the help that's offered. Active self-care is knowing when to accept and receive external support.

Once the grief journey begins with a *Freshman griever,* that person is assigned an Accountability Partner, available whenever the fresh griever needs to share. We take extreme care in aligning the person fresh on grief's trail, with a mother who has been on the journey for at least 3 to 5 years. An Accountability Partner's presence instills hope.

During the first few weeks and months of active grieving, the Accountability Partner is prepped and debriefed to journey with the fresh griever. Sharing scrambled thoughts and "the weepies" always seem less confusing when one can express them to an understanding, empathetic ear. A contingency plan is always available for either of the partners to receive additional support when necessary.

Mothers later acknowledged that despite the conflicting emotional pain they experienced, the presence of a mother who has been on the trail, who has experienced what they have now been involuntarily pushed into, gave some consolation. Many felt that that mother provided an inkling of hope during their storm.

Please note: There might be times when an assigned Accountability Partner cannot journey with a fresh griever. A few scenarios might be at play. There might be times when that person is triggered and needs to attend to her wellbeing; the person might have had a restless or sleepless night and may not be attentive or at full cognitive capacity; a recent incident might have been retraumatizing.

Although everyone should be able to gauge their level of contribution, I check in to provide intermittent debriefs not only for the *Freshman griever* but also to ensure that veteran mothers are also monitoring, taking care of their wellbeing, and identifying areas where they, too, might be needing support.

Fresh grievers are advised to refrain from making any major decisions during this confusing time, which they'll likely, and as experience has proven, later regret. Decision-making for simple day-to-day tasks and self-care are considered standard, but other life-altering decisions should be deferred within the first year of a significant, traumatic loss.

There are those within one's family or household who might exert undue pressure with requests for a fresh griever to take on extra tasks. Please be assertive enough to decline, especially if, as a fresh griever, one feels unwell or incapable of doing what's being asked. Saying no to a request is part of being kind and gentle with oneself. No one can give or produce what one doesn't have the physical or mental capacity to give or do. During these highly stressful and painful times, the main principle is taking care of oneself and being at one's best first, before attempting to assist others.

Sadness and Depression

Among the array of emotions that persist, sadness is at the top. Sadness is the natural sensation which helps us cope with any emotional unrest. Sadness is cathartic and assists in relieving and releasing tension in our bodies, minds, and spirit. Besides helping us express self-empathy, it also balances the emotions around us as we access and assess other family members' pain.

During extreme sorrow, the human tendency is to focus on self, but sadness around us should draw us into a collecting, empathizing space where a family can jointly console and draw comfort from each other. This collective sadness knits the family's strength together in reciprocity, as people needing each other, with a reliable shoulder to lean on. Unlike natural death, traumatic loss radiates excessive pain which must be channelled in a balanced atmosphere, so families can remain cohesive.

Sadness is an emotion that must be shared, talked about, cried over, and explored, to move through the grieving process. As a natural emotion, sadness softens over time, but can also linger to the point where it might evoke feelings of exhaustion, worthlessness, and self-pity. Sadness and depression bear a distinct correlation to each other. Where they differ, however, is in the traits associated with each one. While sadness is normal, healthy, and passes eventually, depression lingers, intensifies the sadness, and creates other unhealthy thoughts and behaviours.

When sadness is prolonged, stirring feelings of hopelessness and hindering activities of daily living, it's an indicator that we must look outside ourselves to external supports, to avoid deep depression.

Depression is also seen as a natural, normal grieving process but can, over time, become persistent and overpowering, creating a downward spiral into mood disruptions, that can turn into clinical depression. Identifying the desire to self-isolate, disassociate oneself from company, experiencing loss of appetite, inability to concentrate, insomnia, deferring important decision-making, and lethargy are significant signs that shouldn't be ignored.

Consultation with a therapist or physician should be seriously considered for the necessary support to resume healthy functioning. Self-talk, sharing with others, and listening to directed supports during these critical times, will help the griever remember that "this too shall pass."

Panic, Fear, and Anxiety

> *"Fear, anxiety...and pain; all are emotions and sensations. They are neither right, nor are they wrong; good nor bad. They are simply [emotions,] a most important part of life. Feel them, fully experience them, surrender to them, and learn to accept them. As a submissive, you must let go."*
> **- André Chevalier**

Emotions run relatively high from the onset of traumatic grief until the initial chaos abates. Panic, anxiety, and fear are among the early emotions as one's mind struggles to understand the chaos around them. Fear for the safety and wellbeing of remaining children will continuously arise. Grievers' own sense of safety will be rattled as they slowly swirl within the clutches of panic.

These are natural body and emotional trauma responses, to which grievers might have been exposed. Some people who are prone to panic attacks, might experience frequent bouts of it. Slow, deep breaths and adequate rest are recommended, even if/when sleep is elusive.

Some people have found it easier to isolate themselves even in their homes. Receding in thoughts is not the safest or healthiest thing to do. Talking, sharing emotions and thoughts are healthy activities which assist grievers in processing disturbing emotions. Music has been proven to soothe the mind and improve moodiness. Sourcing an inspirational song that stirs the spirit can be placed on repeat until the gloominess lifts. I endorse this activity which continues to work for me.

It's also important for grievers to acknowledge melancholic feelings and share them with kind, empathetic listening ears. If the symptoms become more frequent and persist, a session with a therapist or seeking medical help is advisable. Despite current despondent situations, the sun will continue to rise every morning and set in the evening as it runs its course. So too, periods of gloom, dejectedness, and feeling downhearted will run their course. Trauma-laden grievers have weathered the torrents of traumatic grief and found fresh, sunny days, which bring them to the other side of growth and renewed hope.

Guilt, Regret, and Blame

> *"Maybe there's more we all could have done, but we just have to let the guilt remind us to do better next time."*
> **- Veronica Roth, Divergent**

Feelings of guilt are not new to the grieving process. In combination with regret and blame, guilt is among the conflicting emotions which rear its persistent head in the early stages of grief. Robert Bauger (1997) identified eight types of guilt, which vary depending on the circumstance of the death, the people involved, and the level of relationship with the person who died. Among those, he listed "Role Guilt, Survival Guilt, Moral Guilt, If Only Guilt and Recovery Guilt" as playing significant roles in gun violence-related deaths.

If Only Guilt. One survivor I worked with felt sure that if she had gotten home sooner, after leaving work, her son would still be alive.

Moral Guilt. During a group session, another survivor felt guilty about taking another shift to cover for someone else when she could have been at home earlier, at her usual time. Her presence at home would have helped—although the incident happened away from her home.

Survival Guilt. A sibling felt exceedingly distraught and expressed that she should have died instead of her sister, who was much nicer and got along better with their mother.

Role Guilt. Parents have questioned whether they showed enough love, cautioned enough, or were too hard on the child who died.

Recovery Guilt. Every survivor fits into the final bracket. They question what life would look like as they contemplate living without their loved one. Is it possible to even find pleasure in everyday activities? Can they smile, laugh, or even live a normal life with other children after this horrific death?

Although feelings of guilt, regret, and blame are natural parts of grief, particularly traumatic grief, healing and reconciling these emotions are necessary to shift, heal, and find meaning. Like any other emotion, there must be an acknowledgement of the feeling(s). In some cases, survivors can also become stuck if they ruminate on one situation for extended periods.

The fluidity of grief allows us to ride waves of emotions and rest as the waves recede. With the ebb and flow of the tide, we receive welcomed respite where honest reflection and processing of emotions can lead to realization and openness. Any emotion, guilt, blame, regret or otherwise, can be explored, processed, and rephrased, allowing us to pick ourselves up and prepare for renewed, strengthened steps.

Grief has been referred to as the "Master Tutor." Where we can make adjustments in our behaviour, attitude, or interactions, we do so. We can honour our loved one by being kind and understanding with ourselves. Hopefully, when opportunities arise to make positive changes, we'll be wise enough to identify those areas and adapt. Most grievers express how much they learned and grew during their grief journey.

Fractured Communities

Hopefully, all those associated with grief will continue to allow the lessons of grief, loss, and trauma to help us reframe our thinking, and rearrange our actions and attitude, to become better companions on the journey. Between all these learning processes, we discover and recover parts of ourselves that we may have lost, or that laid dormant. We might realize talents, or an affinity to a new activity or hobby; we might even ascertain a particular career, that draws us with a level of conviction that we cannot shake.

During a session with a Survival Guilt sibling, I was pleasantly surprised when she blurted out that she felt the strong desire to become a therapist. Her rationale was that she knew of other siblings who needed support in the areas with which she struggled.

Explosive Emotions

> *"Fear is a very explosive emotion, but it has a short life span. It's the sprint. The marathon is hope."*
> **- Mike Huckabee**

In my nursing days, I became familiar with and understood the term "baby-brain" to mean the sleepless nights and exhaustion that came with a newborn until the baby and everyone else adjusted. While contemplating this book, I felt that the idea of "grief-brain" could also be identified with the grieving process.

During grief-brain, people endure a systematic series of emotional disruptions and make amendments on the psychological level as they seek to adjust to the inevitable life change. (Zisook & Shear, 2009).

Grieving is an explosive experience as we seek to balance the tangled web of heightened emotions. One mother wept as she disclosed how one of her remaining sons "was getting on her last nerve." She confided that she needed to know where he was at all times and if he didn't answer the phone when she called, that her "mind went to the unthinkable." We explored her emotions and drafted a map to track the "when, why, how, and what" of her volatile emotions.

As learning tools for the group, we identified the importance of understanding that our emotions reflect our mental state and reveal the areas in our lives that are of concern. Emotions are simply the feelings, moods, or sentiments that allow us and others to know our temperament. When emotions are continuously explosive, we need to challenge that status quo. Although emotions are biologically based, they are also psychologically induced, depending on the circumstances one experiences.

Emotions tend to run extremely high during grief and trauma as they relate and respond to thoughts, feelings, and pleasure or displeasure. In every situation humanity experiences, we are genetically wired to cope. Humans display happiness when overjoyed and sadness when experiencing emotional pain or distress. Tears flow naturally when we grieve or feel immense sadness. Many feel embarrassed to cry or display sadness.

Whether we are grieving or not, we manage our emotions, and it shouldn't be the other way around, where we have to apologize or feel self-conscious because of emotions.

Although outside the norm, one occasionally expects and hopefully understands the fits of anger, frustration, sadness, and even curtness when dealing with fresh, traumatic grief. We change the circumstance of being explosive by first identifying and acknowledging the emotion. Secondly, by understanding why that emotion or emotions erupt, and third, we seek ways to improve our interactions and successfully shift.

The International Encyclopedia of Psychology (1997) describes emotions as

> "A valence experience that's felt with some degree of intensity, which involves a person's interpretation of the immediate situation, and is accompanied by learned and unlearned physical responses."

During traumatic grief, anyone's immediate situation can be adjusted to "learn and unlearn" reactionary impulses.

It's said that "man is a speck of reason floating on a sea of emotions." That previous mother's interactions with her son improved over time as she slowly and intentionally navigated the ebb and flow of her visceral emotions, to a more reasonable and calmer approach to her son going out by himself, where she knew where he was, and eventually going to events with friends.

Relief and Release

> "And when great souls die, after a period, peace blooms, slowly and always irregularly. Spaces fill with a kind of soothing electric vibration. Our senses, restored, never to be the same, whisper to us. They existed. They existed. We can be. Be and be better. For they existed."
> **– Maya Angelou**

Throughout history, art forms have played a significant role in representing grief where the darkness, wallowing, and "groping in the shadows" that have become well-known to grief, and particularly to the type of traumatic loss that mothers who have lost a child to gun violence experience (Starr, 2015). So too, the art form of rhyme and prose allows us to envision the picturesque relief and release, which accompanies the epilogue of grief, where restoration can be acquired at the death of a loved one, and after the intense traumatic phase of anticipatory grief.

Family members endure excruciating emotional pain witnessing a loved one's suffering and prolonged agony before impending death. Someone who has been diagnosed with a terminal illness, for instance, and is unable to care for themself, would have to rely on parents or other family members for day-to-day care. While most families would be gracious and enduring, the overall psychological strain on a caregiver can be strenuous, even when the duties are shared.

One family sought intermittent therapeutic support and incessantly complained about the tremendous strain they all endured. They readily expressed deep love and concern for that sick family member, but were emotionally, physically, and financially drained from the pressures of providing total care for that member. Palliative care is sometimes available, but few do not qualify, with other barriers that members cannot overcome.

When that family member died, everyone expressed relief that his pain and suffering were over. They expressed relief that they could now readjust their lives and find healing themselves.

Although they missed having that loved one around, they were relieved that his pain was finally over. They were relieved that they no longer had to helplessly watch while he suffered. They were also relieved that their emotional, physical, and financial struggles would diminish. It would take some time for them to adjust and grieve, but they expressed the customary phrase many use, "He is now in a better place."

Oxford Dictionary offers two definitions for "relief:"
1. The act of removing or reducing pain/anxiety.
2. The feeling of happiness that you have when something unpleasant stops or does not happen.

Feeling relief after death is sometimes termed as "the unspoken emotion." While many agree that feeling relief after the death of a loved one who experienced intense suffering is okay or permissible, such expressions are done in low tones or out of earshot. Societal judgment and even remarks from relatives and friends denote disapproval, and suggest insensitivity on the person's part.

One rather unusual incident of a gun-related death received excessive comments from group members when the father of the person who died, openly expressed relief when talking about his son's death. This father tearfully explained that his son's mannerisms had changed drastically over the years. Although he readily expressed love for his son, he was also afraid of him. It was distressing to hear that father reveal how his son instilled fear among family members in the home. He wanted to attend the group for his peace of mind as he framed it. He felt guilty, in a way, and wondered if others would judge him harshly for expressing his relief.

One of our group's guiding principles centres around "mutual respect." Every group member must recognize and expect that there are times when someone will say something that we might not like or agree with. Yet, in congeniality, everyone needs to understand, that that person has the right, just like everyone else, to express their feelings without being judged, criticized, or ridiculed.

The other guideline directly following was *'Maintain Confidentiality,'* with this proverb:

> *When you come here,*
> *What you see here,*
> *What you hear, here,*
> *When you leave here, let it stay here.*

Group members are expected to respect each other's thoughts and know that whatever is said by anyone in the group, is not to be repeated outside of group times. The consequence for betraying this trust is a written apology to the group and a 2-session suspension period. Our main objective is to ensure that everyone who attends feels safe, comfortable, and secure while sharing.

There was a pause as group members processed and quietly accepted what that father disclosed. It was impressive to see a few members approach him with encouragement and audible support. His feelings were validated with understanding, reassurance, and hugs. The elements of *relief* and *release* were demonstrated as we continued the session.

Feelings of relief do not negate the love, or the sadness one feels about the death of a loved one. Mutuality of emotions can be experienced about the same situation or experience, especially when warranted, and that's okay.

A person might love someone and still feel disappointed about their behaviour; they might feel extreme sadness about their death, but also have deep feelings of relief that the anxiety, pain, or fear associated with that person's life has ended. Feeling relieved also releases any heaviness, distress, or anxiety associated with the person's death, allowing the living to process their grief effectively.

Crying is OK Here!

> *"Don't be ashamed to weep; 'tis right to grieve. Tears are only water, and flowers, trees, and fruit cannot grow without water. But there must be sunlight also. A wounded heart will heal in time, and when it does, the memory and love of our lost ones is sealed inside to comfort us."*
> **– Brian Jacques, Taggerung**

During every event, including our training sessions, we make the habitual announcement that "Crying is OK here!" and provide tissues that are visible and accessible.

Tears are the heart's natural response to emotional pain. Grieving is the usual, accepted response to the death and deep feelings of emotional pain that we experience at the demise of a loved one. The pain can be intensely more profound depending on the closeness of the relationship, length of time we spent with, lived with, or knew that special person.

Tears and crying are heartfelt expressions of sorrow and pain. It is not a sign of weakness or self-pity. It takes courage and strength to look after oneself and to actually "feel" the deep sorrow that comes, most times unpredictably, automatically, with the sudden death of someone emotionally close to us.

Tears come freely as the outward result of the heart's attempt to process, express, and incorporate the emotions we feel during "fresh" grief. Fresh grief is generally acknowledged as the period from the onset of death up to one year after the death.

Grieving is hard work. It drains the griever on the emotional, intellectual, physical, spiritual, and social levels. Working through fresh grief requires courage to cry openly; patience to deal with the roller coaster ride of emotions; enough self-compassion to realize that one has no control over the bank of emotions that often threaten to overwhelm; and persistence to keep functioning, when we just want to lay in bed and be motionless.

Tears are the healthy, natural, human reaction of the heart, mind, body, and spirit.

Like a dam overflowing, our hearts find a welcome release from the surplus of emotions that cause our hearts to ache. We are compassionate with ourselves when we allow our tears to flow; we are nurturing ourselves when we give the emotions an outlet to "speak' without words; we practice self-care and self-compassion, when we listen to the spiritual need to cry openly, to let our tears express our deep sorrow.

After the first focus group we conducted at a high school in our community, I said that I was happy to see young men crying openly, actually howling as some sank to the floor in tears. Someone was shocked at my reaction and wondered how I could possibly be happy with that. My happiness wasn't that those young men were sad, but that they found an outlet and allowed themselves to feel, to succumb to the release from years of pent-up emotions. Many of those young men had lost siblings, friends, and acquaintances to gun violence. They were previously adhering to the misguided adage, "real men don't cry."

One youth who participated in our trauma-focused training and graduated as a facilitator hurried out of the room when he noticed some of his friends crying. I rushed after him because I felt he was running away from his emotions. I brought him into a separate room and gently talked him into releasing the clamp he had on his feelings. I advised him on the importance and benefits of getting in touch with, and releasing those emotions. I was touched that he allowed me to journey with him for those brief moments of weeping release.

There's no need to apologize for our tears. Solace, relief, and healing come in gradual succession with each episode of crying relief, sadness, or suffering tears. People accept tears when we automatically cry while laughing; we accept tears of joy when someone is surprised to see a loved one who's been away for a while; we cry happily through graduations, award ceremonies and other happy festivities. Yet, we fail to make room for the necessary tears of sadness and grief.

Researchers have found numerous benefits of crying among which, five are related to grief:

1. Helps to self-soothe
2. Dulls pain
3. Assists one's recovery from grief
4. Restores emotional balance
5. Improves mood

From infancy, crying has been a mode of emotional expression and release. The human heart, mind, body, and spirit desperately needs this outlet, which assists in releasing pent-up emotions, such as anxiety and stress from the body. Most importantly, crying produces healing hormones during suffering and grief, allowing the natural progression of grieving to occur.

During grief, we go through the "weepies" at the mention of the lost person's name or thought of that person induces spontaneous crying. Weepy spells lessen over time, as do the intervals between the need to cry, depending on personality. Over time, weepy episodes become mixed with laughter and fond memories as we reminisce and commemorate our loved ones. When we feel the urge to cry, allow the natural promptings of our bodies and emotions to take the lead. Crying really IS OK!

Measuring and Comparing Grief

I Measure Every Grief I Meet (Excerpt)
*I measure every Grief I meet
With narrow, probing, eyes –
I wonder if it weighs like Mine –
Or has an Easier size.*

*I wonder if They bore it long –
Or did it just begin –
I could not tell the Date of Mine –
It feels so old a pain –*
- Emily Dickinson

We are often guilty of minimizing, dismissing, and comparing grief. Studies have shown that although the universality of grief is a common phenomenon among humanity, every human being from every culture, ethnicity, race, or religion, grieves differently. The idea that grief can be compared is as absurd as preventing the sun from rising in the east.

We often weave poetry, music, and other art forms into training, presentations, and events. Like grief, poetry has the unique ability to evoke emotions and memory; to console and strengthen resolve; it induces self-reflection, and instills a sense of hope to listeners and those who allow themselves to be moved by it. Many grievers have found expressive voices and outlets for their grief through poetry.

Some people have used Emily Dickinson's *"I Measure Every Grief"* to support their premise that grief can be compared. However, a closer look at the poem shows Dickinson's concern for grievers rather than making a comparison. She knows her sorrow, the height and breadth of it, but she's wondering about the sadness in the world, and how everyone's dealing with it, and if their grief "weighs like hers." She further likens pain to an object that can be measured by inches and weight.

Dickinson seems to be comforted in the knowledge that she's not the only one suffering and contemplates the probability that, like herself, some people in the world may, or may not find relief from the sadness of their grief. She resorts to spirituality, observing the universality of the "pain-weight" that everyone carries, and surmises that some resemble her own grief pain. Considering Dickinson's short, precise style of poetry, she seriously contemplated grief, grievers, and grieving in this lengthy, ten-verse, introspective poem.

All grieving persons have one universal thing in common: they have experienced a loss and feel separated from their loved ones. If that loss was sudden and traumatic, it will be named as such, but it doesn't negate the permanent separation from a loved one. It's distressing to admit that there are times when even those who have experienced a traumatic loss, will minimize, dismiss another person's grief. Moreover, some make comparisons, depending on the length of time since an initial loss, or the type of loss someone had.

There is no hierarchy status in grief. Every loss and grief experience is significant and tangible because we are feeling, thinking, and expressive beings.

The variant between loss and the measure of pain or intensity will be different simply because our characteristics are different. The loss itself is simply incidental. We have suffered the loss of separation from someone we loved, someone who was important to us. Neither your grief nor my loss, even though we might use different words to name it or describe it, is less valid, less important, or less recognized.

Grief is a humbling process and an eventuality that every human being must go through, whether king, president, ambassador, or pauper. No gauging or measuring tool can fathom the depth of emotions which accompany a significant loss. Only the persons experiencing the loss know how meaningful that relationship was, and the level of complication accompanying that loss. Only that person can realize the magnitude of such a shattering hurt. We will all thrash around in the murky, uncharted waters of grief and feel our way towards healing.

"You need to respect my grief as I respect yours!" This matter-of-fact comment was made with a distinct emphasis that caused heads to turn in the direction from where it originated. Two people were engaged in what seemed like a heated conversation until that statement signalled a need for others to interject.

Our group was engaged in the usual setup for graduation after training. Emotions usually run high due to the lull in that program that's offered seasonally. Looking at the two people, I realized that one person's loss was a couple of years longer than the other. The person with the long grief journey felt that her loss, which was similar in circumstances, was more important because of the time.

With grief being a tutor, we aimed at seizing every learning opportunity, not only to help keep the peace, but also to enhance healing and promote empowerment. As we coalesced in our circular fashion, centring techniques were necessary to lower tempers and create the space where each one took turns to speak like civilized, empathetic, though grieving beings. It was important for everyone to understand why one person felt that their grief was more significant than the other.

We sought to explore the plausibility of each person's stance:

1. Would the intensity of anyone's grief/loss increase because of time?
2. Was the time, date of grief important in weighing the significance of grief/loss?
3. Is one human life worth more than another?
4. Can a comparison be objectively made between two losses?

Grief's intensity is the same for everyone because everybody will experience losing a significant person in their life. Grief's severity will remain at full capacity, without exception. Although there are different types of grief, no research can identify the magnitude of emotions a griever feels, simply because the grief experience is unique to each of us.

The distinctiveness of grief speaks to the uniqueness of individual loss and the impact it has on every person who experiences it. Each person's relationship with whomever they lost is also different, and only that person can speak to the level of personal loss, taking into consideration the matchlessness of that relationship; the level of emotional connection over time; the length of time, the value of the relationship, and connectedness developed.

Morally, no human life is inherently more valuable or more important than another. Every relationship has its rareness, whether fleeting or long-term. For anyone to feel or think that their grief has more significance than another person's, is simply to devalue that lost person's life and worth as a human being. Furthermore, there is no hierarchy ranking in grief, which chooses to come unexpectedly with its companion, death, at any time or date. Rather than decipher or reason whose grief is more important, we ought to acknowledge and empathize with travellers on the road of grief.

Seeking to make comparisons between grief experiences is as futile as trying to escape death or grieving. Comparing grief or suffering leads to feelings of inadequacies and can only harm ourselves and others.

As we continued to deliberate, both parties conceded to the rationale of 'Grief's work' and the honest truthfulness of devaluing life with comparisons. It is always humbling to be reminded of our frailties as simple humanity, floundering around in our brokenness and grief.

Edith Eger made some profound statements in her book, The Choice: Breaking the Impossible when she wrote:

> "There is no hierarchy of suffering. There's nothing that makes my pain worse or better than yours, no graph on which we can plot the relative importance of one sorrow versus another…This kind of comparison can lead us to minimize or diminish our own suffering" (2017).

The process and task of grieving are gruelling enough without putting undue pressure on ourselves. Instead of making contrasts that belittle us and others around us, we can commit to practicing good, healthy self-care and improved self-talk. We can begin by affirming that:

"We are specialists on our specific journey of healing, and the expert in our own grief."

Various elements such as gender, cultural background, spirituality, social demographics, and environmental issues all play a crucial role in each other's healing journey. We become better pupils of grief, when we acknowledge each other's grief, and work at being empathetic human beings to ourselves. As we show ourselves empathy, we grasp the need to receive kindness, making us more compassionate and willing to extend the same to others.

Understanding Gun Violence and Grief/Trauma Education

An adequate appreciation of any undertaking is a crucial aspect of understanding. Acquiring basic knowledge of any situation provides a framework from which to operate. Educating oneself on the complexities of gun violence is not only vital, but essential to anyone who seriously desires to provide support to victims and survivors. Grief and trauma education hinges heavily on gun violence and its ramifications.

Meaningful response to gun violence demands an unselfish, empathetic view of all the circumstances surrounding that topic, including theories, limitations, complications, and psychological trajectories to everyday living.

From a personal therapeutic point of view, gun violence is a deadly affront to human life with the intent to end a person's existence. Not only does one act of gun violence death end a life, but it leaves a lifetime of agonizing, traumatic effects on individuals, communities, and societies. Due to the demoralizing impact on humanity, this topic demands education from every facet of human functioning.

Therefore, basic education must begin with the lethal aspect of this deadly insult to human life, and the disastrous trail of psychological injuries it entails. Generally, everyone knows and understands the detriment of gun violence. People casually talk about prevention/intervention measures to curb this deadly force, but concrete steps to set a framework are yet forthcoming.

On the community level, education can take the form of alerting students from middle school on the severity of gun violence, while providing warning signs to be aware of and avoid. Prevention/intervention measures should be weaved into the curriculum where high school students are versed on how to incorporate and expand on the basic information outlined in the formative years, starting in middle school.

Students mature at varying levels. During puberty, students gravitate to each other. A less mature student can and might be coerced by peers into unwholesome behaviours related to gun violence. Using Emotional Intelligence (EQ), students can be taught, warned of pitfalls to avoid, and made aware of situations that are termed Prevention/Intervention measures, particularly related to gun violence. Such education should be introduced in elementary school and continued through high school as an alternative subject surrounding safety and security.

The adage *'to be forewarned is to be forearmed'* is critical during these formative years. When one knows of a problem ahead of time, one is better prepared and more alert to avoid it. Early prevention/intervention measures have proven advantageous to students who were forewarned and assertive enough to avoid this pitfall.

I gravitate to Sam Houston's quote, which emphasizes the importance of education, raising awareness, and providing tools for deterrence:

*The benefits of **education** and of useful knowledge, generally diffused through a community, [educational systems] are essential to the preservation of [communities and society].* - (1793-1863)

Educative attentiveness lays the foundation for incremental guidelines, with reinforcement at home and in strategic areas within the community. These platforms are the hinges where socialization and combined intentions are geared towards prevention/intervention.

Specific education related to guns and gangs needs to be emphasized, so high school youth are aware of snares, persons and places that pose a danger to their wellbeing. Youth are very impressionable with varying levels of maturity. Most of them want to please. Succumbing to peer pressure while seeking approval, especially during adolescence, can sometimes be a motivating factor in their need for acceptance.

For many whose identity is intertwined with being accepted, their reasoning can easily be skewed by crafty, unwholesome characters. Education on the consequences of gang involvement with specific attention on 'grooming' techniques, is critical to their overall safety.

Parents are the originators of socialization for the next generation. As parents, we underpin the layout for our children to learn, thrive, and become responsible adults and citizens. Initial lessons in safety begin at home and should continue even when youth start to assert their independence. Youth's advancement processes require that they progress to adolescence/puberty and pre-adulthood. These are natural growth and development areas that, as parents and caregivers, we need to know and prepare ourselves to navigate.

Though anticipated, these expectant stages are very stressful for both youth and parents. Very few fully understand the methodology and the accompanying intricacies inherent to this period in life. Metamorphosis is the transformative progression of a moth > caterpillar > butterfly. Similarly, youth must also gradually detach from parents > gravitate to peers > and eventually find their path to young adulthood and beyond. Many parents are not educated on this process, although they have undergone those stages.

As parents, we enter a state of amnesia when our youth begin to squirm out of their moth-like cocoon towards young adulthood. Logically, the onus is on parental understanding and guidance, which has been very limited in my years of working with both generations. Very few parents understand the need for youth to enter and complete the progressive natural growth and development stages.

Our understanding of this critical area of youth advancement would minimize the anguish parents endure and equally smooth the transition for youth. Knowledge has the inherent advantage of providing clarity which also improves relations during these phases. According to scholars, prevention/intervention measures for parents must also include the testy years of puberty, which ranges from ages 11 to 19. Some scholars differ, citing as early as age 10, while most agree that this age can be stretched to 25 for completion.

Natural growth and development criteria must be understood in tandem with the vulnerability surrounding gun violence. Parents must also be aware of crucial areas and pitfalls threatening disruption in youth experience during puberty towards young adulthood.

A bit of self-disclosure. Being a first responder to crisis, educating others on pitfalls to avoid, and especially providing post-care for survivors of gun violence, I needed to exemplify what I believed and taught. Every Black mother with teenage sons functions in hypervigilance mode whenever their son is not within sight or hearing range.

If my sons were out at 11 p.m., it was a strict rule that they call to let me know where they were and who they were with. I could not sleep until they were safely inside, and I could visibly see that they were safe. Unfortunately, this mental vigilance is prevalent in marginalized communities in Toronto and globally, where gun violence continues to pose a threat.

I made it a priority to continuously talk to my younger son on issues related to gun violence. Part of my regular (daily) routine was keeping a keen eye on his behaviour, language, and attitude. If he used an unfamiliar phrase that I didn't know, I asked open-ended questions to learn. I checked his room for any signs that he might be associating with unwholesome company. I regularly asked if anyone approached him about being in a gang or invited him to participate in any dangerous activities.

If I noticed or overheard anyone suggesting events that seemed suspicious, I cautioned and advised him to disassociate himself from their company. I highlighted public situations of negative youth associations as lessons to be learned. One of my main proverbs back then was *'association breeds contempt.'*

Parents must be vigilant in noticing behaviour changes, including acquiring items and funds that appear out of nowhere or from friends who casually gave these objects. One rule formulated with my sons' input was that they could not accept gifts such as cellphones, brand-name clothes, and other items that we did not provide, except if they had a job and purchased them. Any such gifts or items were not to be accepted or brought home. If they were accepted, our agreement was a prompt return to the person/s who gave them.

Parental directions might be shunned, brushed off, or outright refused, which is why education is essential. Being well-versed in socialization and the key aspects of how bad choices and associations could negatively impact a youth during this growth phase, is crucial in preventing pitfalls and potential death.

Generational gaps often create crevices where youth can easily slip through and become lost. As parents, we must be educated, even if it means educating ourselves, as culture and times change. Granted, many parents, especially in underserved communities, are preoccupied and overtired with two jobs in conjunction with other stressors. Nevertheless, parents must be vigilant and prudent in understanding our current world and the dangers that lurk in coded conversations, on social media platforms, and through sources that threaten overall youth survival.

Parents need to lay a solid foundation of honesty and trust, where children and youth are assured of safety as much as possible, within parental capacity. Youth might put on a bravado, not wanting to give the satisfaction of their parents understanding their anxieties and fears, but they need reassurance just as much as younger children do.

Parental Foresight

A chief by-product of natural growth and development is the rift that is generated between parents and youth. Despite explosive outbursts and intermittent skirmishes, the parent-child relationship is the most significant association during adolescence. Conflicts between youth and parents become more frequent, more intense; youth feel that parents are not supportive and don't understand how they feel. Parents complain of youth being rebellious, disrespectful, and often 'zoning them out.'

Youth development occurs at different stages. Their emotional aptitude is also staggered, and some tend to bloom or blossom later in adolescence. Youth who are overly sensitive will be clingy, will want to hug longer and be held for support. Parents need to be attuned to the youth who need extra attention. These youth will be easily lured into harmful activities, and their 'friends' will take prominent places in their agenda. They will need their space and to be shown respect, but parental awareness is extremely necessary.

Due to the rapid and high-level emotional, biological, and psycho-social changes that youth experience, parental foresight into occurring changes can assist youth to not only navigate their emotions, but also to adapt with a level of flexibility between the ranges of positive and negative emotions. Where healthy attachment was made in a child's formative years, the history of responsive, sensitive interactions with compassionate understanding, helps smooth rough patches, making outbursts and misunderstanding temporary, with limited relational difficulties.

Summary

To date, we have been unable to efficiently deal with gun violence and the trauma associated with it. Even in the 21st century, the reactionary responses to gun violence fall despairingly short of what survivors need.

Globally, Canada ranks fifth on the world stage of gun-related death rates. The United Nations report deaths from small firearms exceeding those from all other weapons combined, stating that more people die each year from gun-related violence than in the atomic bombings of Hiroshima and Nagasaki combined. While the global death toll from the use of guns is estimated as high as 1,000 dead each day, our country's provision for survivors, continues to lack purposeful infrastructure.

The importance of culturally informed practices for gun violence survivors, with trauma-informed practices, needs to be among the actions necessary for judicious responses for survivors. Such fundamental actions will not only be encouraging, but will also be constructive approaches in meeting the complex traumatic needs of survivors.

PART THREE

RELUCTANTTRAVELLERS

Fractured Communities

I walked a mile with Pleasure;
She chattered all the way.
But left me none the wiser
For all she had to say.

I walked a mile with Sorrow
And ne'er a word said she;
But Oh, the things
I learned from her —
When Sorrow walked with me.
Robert Browning, January 1, 1915

A distinctive criterion for OOB facilitators is that they are familiar with funeral homes and their processes. From reactions at previous training over the years, I know it's essential to introduce this in our outline and discuss it during orientation. To reiterate the significance of this principle, our trauma-focused training sessions include a field trip to a funeral home midway through the training. Attendees who have a phobia about funeral homes, and are not ready to objectively participate in a discussion about it, usually drop out after learning that this trip is compulsory.

As the training proceeds, other steps must be taken to alleviate the built-up anxiety often experienced by more than 90 percent of attendees. This specific fear or dread is known as *"thanatophobia"* related to the fear of death, or more precisely, 'fear of the dying process.' The inaugural chapter alluded to the fear of death, and the predictability of this mandatory journey that all living things/beings must take, yet death continues to be a major distressing topic for many.

Life and death walk in tandem with each other. *'In the midst of life, we are in death'* is an appropriate quote from the 1550s, which signifies the duality and contingency of death, as we journey through life. It also profoundly reminds us that the suddenness

Acknowledgements

of death, even during merriment, is also a living possibility. Regardless of this knowledge, becoming familiar with procedures related to death and dying is progressively difficult for us.

Humanity's fear of death intensifies, partly due to social media's portrayal of some grotesque manner of varying circumstances of humanoid demise, and the seemingly integral dread we already display. In my quest to understand these embedded fears, I've concluded that the above-culminated factors, contribute to humanity being 'reluctant travellers' on the grief journey.

Studies indicate that these fiercely entrenched emotions surrounding death and dying, peak by age 20, with another duality within the process of natural growth and development. Youth feel invincible to the point where death cannot touch them—except when it happens—and they must witness the death of another youth.

Thanatophobia affects both genders, although men hesitate, or in some cases, refuse to express those fears. Withheld admission of fears, also contributes to delayed healing, and progressive strides from denial to acceptance. Studies reveal that women in their 50s exhibit and express this type of fear, but are also willing participants, who seek group and professional support to deal with the condition effectively. Parents who never dealt with their fear of dying, when they become elderly demonstrate excessive anxieties, which must be appeased and, where necessary, treated with calming exercises. In extreme cases, spiritual practices eventually provide some respite for those with any faith background.

Reluctant travellers on the grief journey, face enormous complications as they hesitantly work towards healing. Fears already embedded deep within their psyche, must be therapeutically explored and pacified, before they begin the grieving process.

Although children are more easily soothed in most cases, grievers of all ages who harbour this type of fear, endure a much longer journey towards healing. They toggle between the stages of *"denial and acceptance"* for longer than is usually expected, with some delays exceeding six months or more. However, with an understanding therapist or counsellor proficient in grief/trauma, and the many deterrents surrounding the topic, any reluctant traveller can find their way through the grieving mazes to ultimate healing.

CHAPTER 7

CULTURAL SENSITIVITY: AGE, GENDER, TRAUMA, AND CULTURE

"Without mutual knowledge there can be no mutual understanding; without understanding, there can be no trust and respect; without trust, there can be no peace, only the danger of conflict. This means we have to be willing and able to familiarize ourselves with the way people of other cultures think and perceive the world around them, but without losing our own standpoint in the process."
- **Roman Herzog, President of Germany**

Fractured Communities

In 1993, Milton Bennett developed a framework to better understand the stages of *"cultural sensitivity,"* which he initially called "intercultural sensitivity." He hypothesized that people experience insensitivities, and as others become more culturally sensitive—more tolerant—they would progress from having an ethnocentric orientation to a more ethno-relative worldview.

Cultural sensitivity can be termed as the knowledge, awareness, and acceptance of other identities and cultures. I recently found another definition that makes better sense.

> *"Cultural sensitivity is being aware that cultural differences and similarities between people exist without assigning them a value—positive or negative, better or worse, right or wrong."* (Dabbah, 2014).

Dabbah highlighted a simple truth that can resonate with anyone aware enough to acknowledge that with cultural sensitivity, we become aware that people are not all the same, and that our race, culture, or ethnicity is not better than any other culture.

Bennett's "Ethnocentric Stage" theorized that people generally move from "Denial > Defense > Minimization. In his "Ethno-relative Stage"—the stage of awareness where others are embraced—people would make a progressively marginal shift through "Acceptance > Adaptation > Integrating."

According to Bennett's theory, people genuinely interested in embracing cultural sensitivity, make a conscious effort to actually "see" others, not as "different from," but with the cultural sensitivity that integrates differences to find and blend commonalities. Many use the term "cultural sensitivity" and "integration" in sentences that carry a deteriorative tone, that is never missed.

Black and brown people possess an intuitive awareness which raises "the internal red flag" when offensive tones are used,

Cultural Sensitivity: Age, Gender, Trauma, and Culture

making it poignant that, "*They may forget what you said, but they will never forget how you made them feel.*" When we practice cultural sensitivity in our interactions and intentions, we allow the pendulum to shift in our understanding and speech, motives, and behaviours.

Cultural Sensitivity in Trauma

On May 23, 2007, a shudder of despair floated like shock waves through our community. We experienced the first and most alarming gun violence death of the now memorialized youth who had recently celebrated his fifteenth birthday. Amid the usual frenzy of officials, media, reporters, and community members, '*collective trauma*' was quite evident. The unthinkable had happened. Categorized with churches, schools were covertly noted among the sacred spaces in the community, which should be respected and not denigrated.

This had never happened before in a school—a shooting, that is. In the broader community and open spaces, yes. But never in a school.

Situated in the northwest end of Toronto, our community is known as the most diversely ethnocultural neighbourhood in Toronto and Canada. In 2003, the City of Toronto adopted a motto emphasizing equity, diversity, and inclusion as their strength with the publicized slogan: "Diversity, Our Strength."

During that active catastrophe, school officials and other decision-makers scurried about assessing the situation and sought immediate care, first for the victim who succumbed to his injuries and organized support for students and others who needed it. Amid the havoc, a critical element was overlooked, as family members reached out to us for trauma support.

Using '*social stratification,*' one student exclaimed in dismay and disappointment, "They brought 'suits' to talk to us!" In youth culture, particularly in the Black community, "*suits*" refer to someone in power, or in the upper class, who doesn't represent their culture or community, but more ominously, someone who looks down on them.

There's been much discussion about '*social stratification,*' with many questioning whether it's a word or not; or even if it should be used. In urban communities where race, culture, and ethnicity are the bedrock of marginalization, candid deliberations on cultural sensitivity must be encouraged. Society and those in leadership positions must understand the significance of including ostracism in daily interactions and decision-making; while relating to different cultures, and especially in response to traumatic incidents.

"*Ostracism*" refers to the act of ignoring and excluding individuals. It is differentiated from '*social* exclusion,' in that 'ostracism' generally requires ignoring or lack of attention in addition to '*social*' exclusion. By marrying the two words, '*social ostracization*' raises awareness of the importance of looking at the broader picture, and considering, consulting with, and including the specific people for whom care is being considered into the equation.

When providing support for a highly traumatic situation like the incident in 2007, where a youth was murdered, and the entire student body was traumatized, including teachers, "*cultural sensitivity*" appears to have been overlooked. Responding to any intensely emotional and devastating situation, particularly where *diversity* is portrayed in this community, cultural sensitivity should have been one of the highest considerations.

Additionally, gender-appropriate responses, with suitable age deliberation, are not only necessary but highly critical. Cultural adaptation of activities on varying ecological levels is essential when focusing on children, girls, and boys. These are seen as standard intervention measures.

Cultural Sensitivity: Age, Gender, Trauma, and Culture

Although I was a familiar face residing in the community, it took a couple of sessions with some students from that incident, before they were relaxed enough to even want to talk. Realization of the intensity of the trauma, and application of a few cultural sensitivity tips over the years, contributed to establishing a "safe zone." My approach and body language had to coincide with my dialect, and tone of voice to exemplify compassionate trust.

Researchers continue to probe and unearth areas of study which educate, and hopefully assist in creating a paradigm shift in areas where humanity and cultures continue to remain stagnant. With limited research in cultural sensitivity and trauma, Cultural Betrayal Trauma Theory (CBTT) is a contextualized framework created to examine trauma in minority populations (Gómez, 2019). In addition to looking at typically studied abuse outcomes such as PTSD, this culturally focused study also predicts cultural outcomes, such as internalized prejudice, changes in ethnic identity, and (intra)cultural pressures.

"Cultural competence" is another area that is gradually gaining traction.

> *Cultural Competence* is the therapist's capacity to be self-aware regarding their own identities and cultural norms; the therapist's ability to be sensitive to the nuances of the realities of human difference; and the therapist's capacity to possess an epistemology of difference allowing for creative responses to the client. (Laura Brown, 2008).

Grief, and particularly traumatic grief, are individual processes where each person's journey to healing is distinctly unique, where *'gender-responsive, trauma-informed care'* must be included and competently offered.

In conjunction with cultural sensitivity, gender-responsive care must be seen as an obligatory pair to adequately support children, youth, men, and women who all grieve differently. Each gender must be approached with customized relativity.

A child would need reminders about why their brother is not coming home; youth struggling with notions of invincibility need intermittent support. Men who often mask or transfer emotions will be physical with their processing. At the same time, most women, who are generally open with expressing feelings, will participate in groups and open platforms to vocalize their grief and find companionship through healing.

Many have asked whether children grieve. Absolutely! Grief in children starts at a tender age when they're being weaned. Although many have overlooked this critical introduction to grief, children's grief experience covers the areas of initial weaning to parents going back to work after maternity.

The birth of another sibling continues that process, as siblings start school. Beginning at the playground, kindergarten, daycare, or starting school are all grieving processes. Parental relationship break-up or divorce, friends moving away, prenatal illness (i.e., postnatal depression) or parental death, are also included. Children's ability to love is unabashed and unconditional. So is their grieving process.

Loving, stable and responsive relationships are fundamental to children's holistic growth and development. So too is the process of grieving, albeit children grieve very differently than youth or adults. During play-based therapy, a young child can talk, act, express, learn, and grieve. They absorb information and grieve in spurts. The facilitator or therapist must be relaxed and accommodating enough to participate in the play, be open enough to anticipate and respond to intermittent questions, and be alert enough to gather the grief data they provide on a holistic level.

In the middle of playing, it is common for a child to run to you with a grief question, receive a response that resonates, or that

Cultural Sensitivity: Age, Gender, Trauma, and Culture

they accept at the moment, and run back to play. If the response is unsettling, they will repeat the question as they process their grief emotions. They grieve differently.

Youth who feel, express, and act with invincibility, are not exempt from grieving stages and their effects. Losing a friend to gun violence at the height of dauntlessness is not in their consciousness, and does not relate well to youth, according to their macho concepts.

Male youth will respond with anger, ideas of retaliation, and make every effort to conceal their emotions. Most female youth will cry openly, give and receive compassion, share on a one-to-one basis or in a group setting. Male youth try to keep up with the "masculine allusion" society has created, where boys and men must be aggressive, strong, and emotionless. However, when faced with repetitive and relentless gun violence death, many have, over time, participated in activities and supports to alleviate the trauma that they say "won't let up."

Depending on their culture, some men will cry openly, while others will be highly secretive or mask their emotions. Many engage in private, action-oriented expressions of grief alone, but adopt a *macho bravado* in social settings. Others who are physically active would do excessive fitness exercises, distract themselves with a new project, or take up a hobby. Those in high-functioning careers will busy themselves with planning, creating, and implementing new concepts to bury the emotions that haunt them.

Case:

Occasionally, an exceptional grief story dispels the myth that "real men don't cry." On a calm Wednesday at precisely 9:15 a.m., I received a call requesting an urgent appointment at my office. Although I knew this highly accomplished businessman, he would be a new client seeking an authentic professional session at my office.

Fractured Communities

After the necessary documents were signed and we assessed his therapeutic needs, he only had one. He needed the appointment so he could have a space to cry. As he recounted, this gentleman recently lost his maternal grandmother, who was like a mother to him. He could not attend the funeral in another country and could not get over the continuous desire to weep for the tremendous loss he was experiencing.

His wife and children were empathetic, but each time he showed tears, they were quickly halted with "Don't cry; you don't have to cry." Not only was that specific loss tremendous and meaningful to him, as he phrased it, but the sadness he felt at not being able to say a final goodbye was overwhelming. I didn't waste time asking him to tell me about his grandmother—that would come later.

With musical encouragement, tissue, and therapeutic permission, I was physically, mentally, and emotionally present while he grieved in anguish for almost an hour. He identified his need; he allowed room for comprehension and manifestation of his deep sorrow; he sought support and actively engaged in the natural process of grief and emotional pain; he mourned his significant loss and made it personal. I applaud such a strong and responsive approach to grief. Real men do cry, and it is a healthy response.

Community groups, research projects, and events that we conduct, including our volunteer pool, have a wide array of women. Most women are nurturing, emotionally attuned, and outwardly express their emotions and opinion. They talk through their grief, console each other, and harmonize with children who need support, often at their own emotional expense. Occasionally, a few women displayed frustration at having to "expose their private business to others" but later revealed other issues that confused and complicated their process.

Gender-responsive trauma care, which incorporates cultural sensitivity with trauma-focused care, is a critical area of expertise necessary during grief. These components are even more significant when providing care for gun violence victims and survivors. In addition to identity-appropriate approaches to gun violence crisis response and treatment, these measures should be implemented from the onset of trauma, to alleviate future distress to those affected.

Stigmatization with Ramification

Intersecting and influencing all the nuances of race, gender, and cultural sensitivity are the dreaded effects of stigmatization. Racial stigmatization is expressly relevant to youth and highly diverse communities, where a level of entrenched 'self-stigmatization' dogs youth's mentality daily.

> "Stigma is the negative social attitude attached to the characteristic of an individual that may be regarded as a mental, physical, or social deficiency. Stigma implies social disapproval and can lead unfairly to discrimination against and exclusion of the individual." (APA Dictionary of Psychology, 2010).

In recent years, the definition of stigma has been modified dramatically to be more specific, relating to "when someone sees you negatively because of a particular characteristic or attribute (i.e., skin colour, cultural background, a disability, or a mental illness)."

Several distinct components exist in stigmatization, where elements of "labelling, stereotyping, separating, status loss and discrimination occur in a power situation that allows these processes to unfold." (Link & Phelan, 2001). This concept straddles mental health to social stigma, where marginalized youth and communities of colour continue to be racialized. Where youth who already experience and continue to experience "otherness," or are treated "less than," and are even termed as "dangerous, violent, or immoral," these susceptible labels inherently become an association they internalize.

Social stigma is the disapproval of, or discrimination against, a person based on perceivable social characteristics that intentionally distinguish them from other members of society. Such biases not only incite self-stigmatization, but increase feelings of low self-esteem and adoption of harmful coping mechanisms. Black and racialized youths' psychological well-being is seriously impaired by years of repetitive stereotyping, demonstrating behavioural signs of self-stigmatization.

Self-stigma has been deemed as the process in which a person becomes aware of public stigma, agrees with those stereotypes, and internalizes them by applying them to the self (Corrigan, Larson, & Kuwabara, 2010). Studies reveal that people who live with stereotypes attributed to them from the outside world, eventually embody those traits against themselves, which turns into self-stigmatization. These 'identity-based psychological perceptions' can adversely shape an individual's attitude and behaviour patterns, producing decreased self-esteem and increased depression (Latalova, Klara et al., 2014).

Close examination of homicide in Toronto revealed a correlation between Black homicide and the economic disadvantages among large numbers of young Black youth's struggle to obtain residential stability (Thompson, 2014). Black youth also bear most of the victimization from gun violence, which negatively affects Black masculinity, due to the stereotypical slants prompted by gun violence.

These, as well as other ongoing marginalization, merits an approach of cultural sensitivity during traumatic responses. Therefore, mitigating gender and racial difference should include

Cultural Sensitivity: Age, Gender, Trauma, and Culture

an awareness of the disadvantages youth face with insightful, supportive methods.

Along the Zig-Zag Path

Human affinity continues to capture the collective heartbreak of gun violence. A family's reality and community's existence drastically change after an incident of gun-related trauma. Shooting occurrences rarely happen without injury on all levels of human existence. Death is the dramatic and ultimate ramification of gun violence with extensive rippling impacts. Where death is the result, the zig-zag trail of multifaceted complications pushes affected persons into the chaotic terrain of uncertainty, distress, and psychological trauma.

Elizabeth Kubler Ross theorized the initial five stages of grief in her internationally ground-breaking book, On Death and Dying (1969). Ross pioneered the jagged path of grief, initiating that grief is not a linear process—it does not progress along a straight line. From my years of working with various grievers, I've come to believe that the 'zig-zag' adaptation of grief's process is grief's accommodation of human nature. Just as no two human beings behave the same, grief response or adjustment is equally unique to each person.

Zigzagging along traumatic terrain, speaks to the many twists and turns to healing and productive functioning. Complications within our natural framework, including our culture, ethnicity, circumstances, family history, and associations, can also negatively impact our grief journey. Personal philosophy throws an added spoke in our trauma wheel, creating additional curves which must be maneuvered.

It's along these zagged paths that we discover and re-experience ourselves, and excavate buried or obscured talents. These hidden gems are re-birthed, and inspiring, spurring us on from death to rebirth. Other significant gems are the grief-buddies who become life-long friends, acquaintances, and empathizers of our predicament.

The acclaimed, influential poet William Blake, captured the universality of human plight with his poem *"On Another's Sorrow."*

> *Can I see another's woe,*
> *And not be in sorrow too?*
> *Can I see another's grief,*
> *And not seek for kind relief?*
> **- William Blake, "Songs of Innocence," 1789**

Unconstrained by boundaries, Blake's rhetorical question evokes a widespread response that every human knows. Humanity instinctively responds to a smile, a hug, or a gesture of kindness. Likewise, painful emotions such as tears, suffering, anxiety, and trauma stir similar cords of compassion and need no articulation. The scattered few might cynically take Wheeler Wilcox's age-old adage out of context and quote:

> *"Laugh, and the world laughs with you; Weep, and you weep alone; For the sad old earth must borrow its mirth, But has trouble enough of its own"*
> **-Ella Wheeler Wilcox, "Solitude," Poems of Passion, 1918**

Yet, others like Blake, can identify with human pain and affirm human woe. Empathizing with others in the face of adversity extends the pity that Blake's poetry lavishly spreads to the grieving. Treatment we hope to receive on our zig-zag path to healing and restoration.

Cultural Sensitivity: Age, Gender, Trauma, and Culture

Summary

> *"We cannot seek achievement for ourselves about progress and prosperity for our community…Our ambitions must be broad enough to include the aspirations and needs of others, for their sakes and for our won."*
> **- Cesar Chavez, Civil Rights Activist**

Poets and authors employ colourful adjectives to portray the solitary, zig-zagged trail which characterizes grief, loss, and trauma. Quotes, poems, and descriptive languages give life to this melancholic period of human reality, with mysterious yet resonating connections. Whether one is new on the trail, or has become accustomed to the tell-tale signs on the terrain, grief and trauma's bumpy journey constantly demands a fresh look, with an in-depth understanding of each situation.

Although every circumstance requires our attention and empathetic response, the zig-zag edges paint a personalized story unique to those immediately affected, those on the outskirts, and those who engage the traumatized.

Each traumatic incident compels responders and those involuntarily touched to put themselves in another's place. We are challenged to adopt Blake's outlook, where empathy mingles with customized care. Folks are also encouraged to envision the off-hand possibility that we might be in such a position. Depending on your geographical location, this might not be farfetched, although each situation will be uniquely different.

Our approach to human suffering paints its picture. Much like Blake's poetry, our empathy level registers on the universal humanity scale, to indicate a grade that speaks volumes of our range of compassion. Swiss psychiatrist and psychoanalyst Carl Jung felt that the collective unconscious profoundly influences individuals' lives. A universally combined hope can envision

Blake's poem within the constructs of 'humanity,' where, as people who will inescapably experience sorrow, we might empathize and divide each other's grief.

CHAPTER 8

MEANING-MAKING & LEGACIES

"In some ways suffering ceases to be suffering at the moment it finds a meaning."
- **Viktor Frankl, Man's Search for Meaning**

DRAWING ON PSYCHOLOGICAL THEORY AND personal experience from being in a Nazi concentration camp, Austrian psychiatrist Victor Frankl, highlighted the profound role that *'meaning-making'* plays, not only in sustaining psychology, but in the face of intense adversity and trauma. During personal difficulty, Frankl experienced the transformative power of tapping into the innate resilience that all humanity has been gifted with, to emerge more insightful and resolute in his quest to explore human psychology.

Scholars argue that trauma is subjective to the individual's interpretation of any event. While one person might consider an emotionally charged event or circumstance to be traumatic, another person could downplay that same event, which to that person may not be regarded as traumatic. How an individual constructs their worldview, has a far-reaching effect on that individual's life and behaviour. (Parks, & Folkman, 1997).

Park's meaning-based theory of trauma argues that distress due to traumatic life events, result from the violation of an individual's global beliefs and goals (Park & Folkman, 1997). Categorizing 'Global meaning' as an individual's general orienting systems and views of collective situations, Park's concept of meaning-making includes understanding and reinterpreting any traumatic situation in a different way, to rearrange one's core beliefs and goals. Once core beliefs are not violated, re-orientation will help regain control (Park, 2010).

Of all the traumatic circumstances and incidents that have desecrated beliefs and bewildered humanity, gun violence has, by far, outranked them all. I find it difficult and near impossible to envision discrepancy, where anyone can minimize the level of trauma emerging from gun violence occurrence, injury, or death. Disorientation from gun violence trauma, fresh or latent, super-exceeds daily stressors, and rocks the very core of the human psyche. When human beings cannot find rhyme or reason in any given situation, they automatically resort to the word *'senseless.'*

Numerous shooting incidents have been deemed *'senseless,'* particularly when a stray bullet kills a 12-year-old, when a 10-year-old walking the street with his family is fatally shot, or when the person killed has no affiliation with violence or guns in any capacity. These incidents are exceptionally difficult for family and close associates. Meaning-making for parents, siblings, and immediate family members is extremely problematic. Initial therapeutic measures are mainly to establish equilibrium and lay a thin yet solid foundation for reaffirmed safety. Meaning-making for these family members can take upwards of 3 to 5 years.

In some cases, a handful of survivors have become so disillusioned and uncaring after gun violence loss, that after 15 years, some remain withdrawn, isolated, and disengaged.

Frankl reinforced that *"…the meaning of life differs from man to man, from day to day and from hour to hour. What matters, therefore, is not the meaning of life in general, but rather the specific meaning of a person's life at a given moment."*

Attempts at stabilizing a 'freshman' mother's equilibrium are simply making an effort. In the second year of loss, one mother later explained that her hearing seemed impaired. She could hear words, but an echo shrouded them, making it impossible to grasp the meaning. This mother felt "like Alice in Wonderland but in a bad way," as she formulated it. She thought that she was beyond confused and that it took excessive energy to seek clarification.

Within the years of working in this field, I have only witnessed one remarkably outstanding mother who broke the ceiling of attainment. This mother initiated meaning-making with a combined activity for legacy building.

Although I applaud her accomplishments, this achievement came at the detriment of her psychological wellbeing. Her emotions were stifled; she evaded all thoughts about the funeral and others related to the death; she busied herself with activities to the point of exhaustion. Her health failed in various areas, and she was diagnosed with panic disorder and a few other ailments before the end of the first death anniversary.

Even after eight years, this mother periodically experiences episodes of meltdowns and anxiety attacks, which debilitates her to the point of having to be on bed rest for a few days.

Meaning-making is the process of healing towards growth and subsequent empowerment. The hallmark of meaning-making is turning adversity into advantages. One can take a candid look at the situation—in this case, gun violence traumatic loss—and glean nuggets of positives from moving steadily towards healing.

Making-meaning from gun violence loss requires a tremendous amount of small, courageous, and measured steps, from the onset of trauma to gradual healing. A key component in this equation is the relationship between the mother and the lost child. Where there was a strong bond of closeness, the process lengthens to make space for phased healing, before any meaning can be formulated.

Exploration of thoughts and feelings surrounding the fatal event is a significant factor, which can become gigantic stumbling blocks. The period of mourning that loss is also different for everyone. Scholars have mapped out a process for "post-traumatic growth," which implores a closer look at attaining meaning-making.

While these identified steps are remarkable goals that grievers aspire to, they must certainly be seen through different lenses when dealing with gun-related trauma, which produces enormous setbacks, impeding the processes that precipitate meaning-making. A lengthy list of variables plays a significant role in attaining or hindering the process of post-traumatic growth.

The intensity of the trauma, the extent of the loss, type of relationship, subjective characteristics, extent of the traumatic event, and cultural sensitivity, all play a critical role in how healing occurs, and how a survivor moves towards post-traumatic growth.

Included among each process for "post-traumatic growth," are identifiable challenges our research has encountered over the years, with survivors of gun-related trauma.

a) **Greater appreciation of life.**
   - From the onset, this is difficult for fresh grievers—the first year of loss—to envision, especially if the lost child was the only son or if other issues influence the already charged situation.
b) **Appreciation for, and strengthening of remaining close relationships.**
   - Mothers generally become fiercely protective of remaining children, even at the risk of their health, which often defeats the purpose. Siblings feel smothered, and resentment builds. Tensions develop between existing friendships, and silence replaces otherwise vibrant relationships, especially at home.
c) **Grasping awareness of personal strengths.**
   - Many would attest that their strength is diminished in the early stages of loss, with a daily battle against exhaustion and other physical ailments which compound the situation.
d) **Increased spiritual participation and development.**
   - Those who have not lost their faith, affirm that reliance on their Higher Power provides some courage and hope, while others become increasingly angry at the Source of power who failed to keep their loved one alive. Depression and despair replace optimism.
e) **Focus on personal and creative growth.**
   - The catastrophic shock from the harrowing experience limits creative energies at first. Very few survivors can think clearly, and although journaling is advised, the majority complain of jumbled thoughts and powerlessness to make sense of their thought processes.

Gun violence trauma affects individuals and communities in unpredictable ways, erupting diverse responses. Although the above strategies are intended for survivors, many survivors are repeatedly exposed to recurring trauma and retraumatization, which reduces the progression of incremental change, and disturbs any healing that could occur. Meaning-making does not and cannot organically materialize.

Clusters of different responses can emerge from the same traumatic event, making it quite challenging to initiate structured therapeutic processes. An intentional effort is usually required with active engagement. This creates an identified gap in services for those affected by gun violence trauma.

Sharing Your Personal Journey

> *"**Give sorrow words**; the grief that does not speak knits up the o-er wrought heart and bids it break."*
> **– William Shakespeare (Macbeth, 1606/07)**

An enigma exists in grief and among grievers. It can be glaringly true for some, yet quite subtle for others. While some grievers want to share their story and even listen to others talk about their lost loved one, some busy themselves with any and everything to avoid talking. However, healing occurs through sharing one's story. Knowledge is gained, and the release of pent-up emotions transpires. Sharing one's journey is the initial step to healing.

During our volunteer and facilitator's training sessions, a mother who lost a child within the first year is invited to share her story with active listeners. Including a primary story during training allows trainees to hear, first-hand, how a significant loss has wounded a survivor. They are privileged to witness the anguish and listen to the mother's encounter with trauma.

Meaning-Making & Legacies

One mother was prepped and advised to start her story from wherever she chose to begin. I usually have a briefing with the survivor to assess her condition and remind her that as a therapist, I would be there to support, interrupt, or even halt her sharing if she became overwrought. As the primary person in her specific grief/trauma, she was advised to stop whenever she felt she couldn't continue.

Being the chief on-looker of her own grief, a survivor-mother has critical information that only she is privy to. No one can tell her what she's feeling, experiencing, or what she needs to soothe her pain. She is the expert in her grief, and I emphasize this critical fact to her and the trainees.

Someone telling their trauma story is offered a comfortable chair to sit or choose not to sit, preferring to pace. Generally, mothers love to share their stories, although it is a painful process. Some are hesitant and even reluctant at first, but an opportunity to talk about their son, daughter or significant lost person is meaningful and impactful. To prevent grief-stifling, I emphasize the importance of sharing early on the grief journey—preferably after 2 to 3 months.

If one is not a trained facilitator and unfamiliar with traumatic grief, it's advisable not to push anyone into sharing their story. It is also imperative to respect someone's wishes and not coerce them into sharing, especially if they aren't ready. One can occasionally prompt someone into sharing, but always be respectful and understanding if the person is unwilling, or has expressed a desire not to participate.

Sharing one's grief is a bewildering gift both for the person sharing and to the listeners. It carries tremendous benefits from both angles as well. Someone who has been psychologically wounded, and feels that their heart has been shattered by that loss might fumble initially. Still, sorrow always finds words to express its pain, with positively noticeable results. After one mother shared—two months after her loss—she reported sleeping soundly for the first time since the funeral.

During debriefing the following day, she recounted some positive, holistic sensations she experienced. Her first realization was hearing her own voice, 'in a sort of monotone' as she described it. Not only was her awareness heightened, but she was able to identify the areas where her voice was cracking with emotions. This mother felt that she underwent an out-of-body experience during her sharing. Even during the funeral, seeing her son's body in a casket and being buried, she had been struggling to believe or accept that he died.

But as she shared her story, comprehension made room for reality to creep into her awareness quietly; language was prompted to expound with pristine clarity, which her receptive heart needed, to make that shift. No prodding or coaxing could produce the quiet acceptance she displayed, although she knew that her traumatic journey was just beginning.

This is not uncommon for any type of loss in the early stages, particularly if the loss was traumatic and unexpected. This mother felt that she was talking to herself during that sharing. In her exact words, she "gave herself a message, and she received the message." What was her message to the subconscious self? Her son was shot. She saw him in the casket, witnessed him being buried, and she went home and left him there. There was no mistaking that he was dead, and although her heart was breaking afresh, she got the message amid convulsing sobs.

Cathartically, this was a colossal breakthrough for this mother at two months, predominantly for gun violence trauma. Up to that point, I had never witnessed such an early realization or shift. This client had many subsequent setbacks during her journey, but her perseverance in sharing her story contributed immensely to her ongoing healing.

It is vital that sharing any traumatic story be done in a safe, encouraging, and supportive environment. Sharing one's story breaks the 'code of silence' and releases survivors from a silent world of isolation. Body aches and pains are relieved; sleeping habits gradually improve; the mind is slowly being freed and receptive to re-storying difficult areas of the trauma narrative.

Unhelpful and unhealthy areas of the story are slowly corrected; senses become more attuned to compassion and empathy from others; depression, which is the chief symptom for traumatic grievers, becomes less frequent and daunting; intermittent consideration for holistic care is slowly broached and encouraged.

These and other psychological benefits from sharing one's story lay fresh markers that the psyche can cultivate on the healing journey. It is critical to remember that each person's grief journey and healing processes are different, and no two experiences can or should be compared.

Constructing Legacies

> *"…What loss does to the human heart… it lowers our heads and deepens our sorrows, and yet how, in the end, it miraculously restores us. When great trees fall, we weep in unity with the forest—and we rejoice at the legacy that lingers."*
> **- Cicely Tyson, Just as I Am**

Dwelling on his 3-year struggle for survival in different concentration camps, Frankl stressed that "the will to meaning" is the basic incentive for human life. Among the most heart-wrenching conditions to search for, or even hope to find meaning to, is a gun violence death. Very few survivors are remotely able to view their life or surroundings with eyes that can see past their current circumstance to anything more than what they're experiencing. Frankl not only embraced his suffering, but sketched an altruistic roadmap for survivors of extreme suffering to follow.

Makeshift memorials are instinctively erected in areas where sudden death has occurred. They make the unabashed assertion that bears witness to existed lives. Symbols depicting memorialization emphasize that life or lives were suddenly smothered. These testimonials are exhibited on street corners, light poles, benches, intersections, or wherever the demise transpired.

In recent times, those improvised memorials have invaded the peripheries and entrances to government buildings and places that govern communities, cities, and society. Oddly, even in protest, humanity extends tolerant yet quiet acknowledgement, which these impromptu images epitomize. A life was removed. Lives lived—presumed prematurely eradicated—demand validation.

Makeshift memorials assert two distinct statements. First, they insist that respectful recognition be given to attest the humanity of that life. Secondly, they stress the apparent or perceived notion that an inhumane, unjust act has been committed. As flowers wither from these ad hoc formations, aroused emotions, with realization, are compelled to reflect on the fragility of life. Refreshed over time, they receive quiet tolerance as the chimes of time march on.

Families, particularly mothers who lose a member to gun violence, continually express an ardent desire to create an enduring activity as a legacy in that lost person's name. Legacies are fundamental to human existence. Not only do they sanction meaning to life, but they personify the innate desire of the human spirit to survive, thrive and evolve. Deep within the cinders of enduring pain and trauma, the human essence shrieks for creativity and a reason to not just live, but to forge ahead with resolute strides.

On hearing the word 'legacy,' thoughts automatically shift to belongings, inheritance, and accomplishments. Legacy ought to, and generally evoke views on the spectrum of life, living, dying, and all the emotions which constitute humanity.

Meaning-Making & Legacies

Constructing legacies have become the spark from which many broken, demoralized spirits find a ray of light through the ashes of destructive trauma. Hearts constricted by grief, trauma, and perpetual pain have found *'legacy constructing'* to be the pillar that allowed them to emerge as a caterpillar, slowly but steadily from its cocoon. Emergence will differ with each individual and ethnicity, just like the uniqueness of the grieving process. They're also diverse in timeframe, activity, or chosen event.

One dominant theme remains the prime focus. That activity or event must be named for, and represent the person being remembered.

Memorialization is a critical part of the grieving process, which provides an opportunity to remember and cherish fond memories of the lost person, while allowing the family to grieve, create a legacy and, most importantly, heal. Activities such as planned gatherings, games, festivals, scholarships, and annual tournaments are among the many legacies that we have assisted mothers and families to create.

One 'legacy' requested by the mothers of two fallen youth in a double-shooting, has been held successfully for seven years. This event—OK Tournament— done in partnership with other community agencies, incorporates basketball and other games, where teams of youth vie for a coveted trophy that remains with the moms after each event. A full day of activities includes a brief reminder of the importance of individuals, community, and the commemoration of lost lives. Games, food, memorabilia, and activities encapsulate this social yet healing legacy.

The event's evolution draws upwards to 600 attendees and includes most of the safety agencies in our community. Repeating the names of those lost youth and providing a scholarship for post-secondary education to two deserving youth in their names, are the highlights of this annual event. Such an endearing legacy reminds the community of the significance of promoting safety and healing.

It's a bittersweet event. Mothers would rather have their sons present than participate in a legacy bearing their names. Nevertheless, the impact that this legacy of remembering has on the mothers and immediate family is astounding. Surrounded by the community, they are supported, encouraged, and validated in their loss. Each event promotes incremental healing and increases their sense of satisfaction, knowing that their sons' names are expressed and venerated.

Summary

A slow recovery is the most common response to gun violence trauma simply because attaining healing for trauma-related grief is a complicated process which differs for each person. While meaning-making can be achieved over time, it meanders between adjustments and relapse, with fluctuating emotions, where survivors complain of feeling that they are "losing their minds."

Constructing legacies necessitates community participation. Mutual experiences generate a high level of collective consciousness, where traumatic efficacy can benefit affected people. Close observation has revealed strong indications that communities experiencing high rates of repetitive gun violence, must view and remedy trauma, not solely on an individual level, but also on a communal spectrum.

The collective synergy and combined human resources build a robust social fabric, where creative expressions and comradery lessens stress, relieves apprehension, and promotes healing.

CHAPTER 9

RECONCILED IMPLEMENTATION

During these ever-changing times, we must consistently customize and implement strategies informed by lessons learned during crises, to effectively reconcile the trauma that communities endure. Providing culturally adaptable services must be the motivating and responsive approach to on-scene response, and post-care, for gun violence victims and survivors.

Client-focused responses need to be relevant to time, history, and the global awareness which continues to be raised. Society must be open to new ideas, considering all variables. With a highlight on cultural sensitivity, our outlook must also shift to meet these painful and traumatic challenges. Tailored strategies must now encompass age-old remedies and adaptive measures, where cultural competency is weaved into approaches.

Whereas methodologies were enacted without client or community input, stricter measures must include discussions and consultations with youth, families, and communities on lived experiences to determine what they see as relevant to their circumstances.

At the beginning of the twentieth century, researchers started to earnestly probe into the concept of conferring with, and including cultural competency into crisis response. Some felt that attention should be placed on cultural values and traditions, linguistics and literacy, immigration experiences and status, help-seeking behaviours, cross-cultural outreach techniques and strategies, including avoidance of stereotypes and labels (Athey & Moody-Williams, 2003).

In diverse communities where the multiplicity of culture intersects, much more needs to be done to not only understand, but engage with patrons who comprehend their precise needs, and what would assuage situations related to their care. Deliberation during and after traumatic events are often considered to be shocking, drastic, and inhumane (Eyerman, 2019).

Race and culture shape how trauma is experienced, especially those whose lives and conditions make them unwitting prey to these ongoing events, including witnessing and being injured by gun violence. Through consistent engagement with youth, mothers, families, and communities, many affirm that their post-homicide experiences are grounded in social and cultural complexities which shape their resilience trajectory (Bailey et al., 2015).

A couple of years before virtual sessions became mandatory, I worked with a soft-spoken youth who was petrified to leave his home to attend therapy. He was shot by a stray bullet that required three weeks in intensive care and hospitalization for a couple of months. After much coaxing, this young man in his 20s, accompanied by his mother, hesitantly ventured out for his first face-to-face session, which was extremely tense.

He was sweating profusely, and his breath was laboured. Although he was in a building with a police division across the street from us, he kept nervously glancing over his shoulder, in hypervigilance mode. It was well over another month before he dared to come out again for his second face-to-face session. Three months later, after patient sensitivity, his hyper-alertness subsided.

My work with another youth going through the initial trepidation of leaving his home was subsequently assisted by the first youth described above. He eloquently and with a bit of dramatics appeased the fears that subsequent youth was facing. He expressed gratitude that someone showed sensitivity, who understood the community, with the fears surrounding the issues of gun violence.

These youths' experience necessitated a modification to our post-care for youth who were injured by gun violence. Adaptability in arranged approaches must be flexible to assimilate with person-centred, ongoing changes as they occur. Tailored services must be smartly integrated with positive strategies to enhance survivors' care and healing processes.

When Life Doesn't Make Sense

> *"Life doesn't make sense without interdependence. We need each other and the sooner we learn that, the better for us all."*
> **- Erik H. Erikson**

Detecting the sounds from gunfire for the first time can be described as surreal and weird but can also be mistaken for other sounds such as firecrackers or fireworks. Although it sounds like firecrackers, our minds want to believe that it is something else.

My first encounter with *'the gun sound'* dismissed the "fight-or-flight" hormonal warning that this might be 'the acute stress response' and ran toward the sound. Instinctively, I feared that someone might be shot and precious time to intervene or save a life might be wasted.

With incredulous relief, I later found out that a first-time gun user had missed the intended target, but I met a 7-year-old who was petrified with shock. He obviously wasn't instructed to lay low when these sounds erupted but was aware enough to know from where they originated. I grabbed him to a secure corner and crouched with him as we waited for silence. After I regained my composure, I pondered the statement which that shocked child kept repeating. *"It doesn't make sense. It just doesn't make sense."*

What exactly doesn't make sense? Why would a child as young as seven think that this doesn't make sense? How could I possibly explain this incident so it might make a bit of sense to him—to me? I pondered on the cartoon with Charlie Brown and Lucy, dwelling on the familiar phrase Lucy uses **"Good Grief Charlie Brown!"** and felt that that would be an excellent place to start. But I would need to find out what exactly didn't make sense to him first. I ruminated over that child's bewildered comments and audibly agreed that it didn't make sense!

It doesn't make sense that youth have easy access to handguns. It doesn't make sense that most shooting deaths are happening in marginalized communities. It doesn't make sense that young Black men account for the majority of deaths associated with gun violence. It doesn't make sense that these young men's lives are being snuffed out by other young men their age. And no, it definitively doesn't make sense that I had to scramble to find a reasonable response for this frightened child, whose innocent mind seeks to find reason amid the unreasonable.

Crisis in marginalized communities is interlaced with sporadic periods of calm. One never knows if, when, or from where something adverse might happen. Communities like ours experience various levels of inequities. Multi-layered barriers of socioeconomic circumstances, normalization of trauma exposure, and the transgenerational impact of trauma are among the daily stressors that marginalized communities face. Hearing gunfire, or that someone was shot, and worse, that someone was killed in the community, is an upsetting reminder of the dangers of being 'home.'

Research shows that guns remain the leading cause of death for young Black men. Shooting has long been the most common cause of death in homicide cases worldwide, with slightly more than half of all homicides being carried out with firearms, according to the UNODC (United Nations Office on Drugs and Crime), 2019. One certainty is that gun violence is within the fabric of repetitive, damaging incidents expected to happen within every Black, marginalized community.

Where Do I Fit in?

> *"Genuine feelings cannot be produced, nor can they be eradicated… the body sticks to the facts."*
> **– Alice Miller**

Reminding survivors of gun violence that they are the expert in their own grief, is a critical point which must be continuously reiterated. All trauma survivors and grievers must understand this simple sentence. When a griever enters the 'tunnel of grief,' the only way forward is *through it*. There can be no turning back. As much as we would like to change a circumstance or incident of gun violence death, we are limited in our wish or desire to turn back the hands of time.

Fractured Communities

There are days when one feels they don't fit anywhere. One might even question one's very existence. This thought, feeling or reaction, again, is not uncommon. Grief's purpose is to help us redefine who we are as we heal, grow, find meaning, and return to a new normal.

In our fast-paced world with unending technological gadgets, most of us seldom take the time for self-discovery. Very few of us understand our identity and the many facets of our traits. For some of us, our identity is wrapped up in a spouse or significant other, where we allow our lives to pale in that person's shadow. Grief's journey is painful, yes, but its primary purpose is to help us redefine who we are and find our place in the world, whether it's in our family, profession, or otherwise.

Our bodies remember and remind us of days, dates, and times when our conscious minds are too threadbare to remember.

I awoke one October morning feeling deeply depressed. My head was aching, and I couldn't shake the feeling of being in deep emotional pain. With my therapeutic hat on, I tried to recall what I had seen on TV the night before; I ruminated about who I had spoken to—an overly disturbed client perhaps—but all checkpoints were clear. What could be precipitating this depression?

As my mood continued to plummet, the name Rochelle popped into my mind. It was October 22. Rochelle's birthday. She would have been 19 that day. I didn't remember, but my body did. As the surge of tears flowed, I allowed my mind to relive the agony of remembering. Rochelle was one of the babies I lost. She was delivered full-term but died after delivery. I held her, counted her tiny fingers and toes before the nurse took her away for an autopsy. Being a nurse, I was very familiar with the procedures, which intensified my loss.

Time seemed to suspend as the day slowly dragged on. I re-experienced that piercing loss with fresh, disquieting memories.

Throughout that day, I entertained the thoughts of regret, foreboding and what-if's but had to prepare to do my trauma-focused training that night. It was sobering and humbling to include my personal story in that training session. Sobering because it was a personal disclosure, and humbling because I knew that although my account might trigger some attendees, it was necessary to demonstrate being comfortable enough with my grief to allow life and duties to continue.

I give thanks that I was sufficiently healed and composed enough to deal with the situation and moved forward with grace.

One of the landmarks inside the tunnel of grief is the identity benchmark. We might find ourselves questioning our emotions and even feel that we don't know who we are anymore. As humans, we possess an individual identity, a human identity, and a spiritual identity whether we have faith, a belief, or not. Holistically, we function on all those platforms. Grief's tentacles will extend to all those areas in varying degrees. We will feel bewildered through our physical, professional, financial, relational, and spiritual identities and in our overall outlook. Traumatic grief can force us to rethink who we are and our identity factors in the various arenas.

Gun violence death stirs consciousness and shakes assumptions of our world, evoking negative feelings of withdrawal, pessimism, jadedness, and disinterest in social activities or detachment from others. Traumatic grief pushes us to the crossroads of life, where we understand that in the face of extreme loss, some things pale in significance and are replaced by others that bear more prominence. Our resistance to change must also be re-evaluated. Nothing before that loss will ever be the same. We, ourselves, will be forever changed, as will our outlook on life, along with our social, personal, and spiritual identities.

The favourable news is that we become wiser and hopefully share our newfound knowledge with others who are fresh on the trail.

Fractured Communities

Summary

"Safety and security don't just happen; they are the result of collective consensus and public investment. We owe our children, the most vulnerable citizens in our society, a life free of violence and fear."
- Nelson Mandela, Former President of South Africa

During these sculptured moments, we confront a time in which lives are deeply affected by gun violence trauma, and families face tremendous life-altering challenges. These intensely painful threats must be met with a blend of age-old remedies and customized strategies informed by lessons learned during ongoing crises. Such lessons can be adapted into best practices.

Gun violence has become so rampant that one can expect to hear actual sounds at any time or see gruesome depictions in the media. When a 7-year-old is caught within the range of active gunfire, our hearts and minds must be disparaged. Nonetheless, these are the conditions within marginalized communities that experience continual gun-related injuries and deaths.

For every gun-related incident, even without injuries, a minimum of 130 people are affected. Those within the hearing range are included in the immediately affected parties, such as extended family, close friends, schools, churches, groups that the person might belong to, other acquaintances and the local community. With our expansive technology, reports and media releases penetrate a broader scope and extend beyond national boundaries to the global arena.

The necessity to address gun violence trauma is increasingly seen as an essential part of effective behavioural healthcare, and an integral part of the healing and recovery process. The repercussions of traumatic events place a heavy burden on individuals, families, and communities. Attention must also be placed on the psychological impact such occurrences have on children who are bewildered, not only by the sounds of gunfire, but on the injuries sustained and resulting deaths.

PART FOUR

HOLISTIC OVERVIEW

Fractured Communities

"Just as the body goes into shock after a physical trauma, so does the human psyche go into shock after the impact of a major loss."
- **Anne Grant**

GUN VIOLENCE HAS BEEN AND continues to be an unrecognized epidemic, creating high rates of homicides and lifelong grief-related trauma in marginalized communities. This gun epidemic continues to weaken families as well as community frameworks.

Recently, a veteran mother, who lost her son to gun violence 20 years ago, talked about her 'good days' when she can smile, laugh, and even talk about her son without the weepies. In the same breath, she muttered, "but...the bad days are really bad!" Those bad days are times of excessive sadness when she feels distraught and embittered. On those days, she's incapacitated, haunted with nostalgia, as she broods over the hopes and dreams she lost on the fateful day her son was killed.

It is an atrocious falsehood to state that people bounce back from gun violence trauma. There is no "bouncing-back" from gun violence trauma. Many families and mothers cannot seem to find their way out of the obscurity which entraps them.

It has been well documented that any trauma has an indelible impact on the human psyche. However, gun violence and its deadly effects become so deeply embedded in human memory that it imprints inescapable imagery that is often irreversible. With years of therapy, these images fade in intensity and can slowly be replaced by re-storying. But the fears, anxieties, and phobias developed from the onset of trauma remain with survivors.

Researchers like Dr. Bessel van der Kolk determined that trauma induces physiological changes, which produces a heightened state of anxiety, and re-experiencing the trauma, which feels real and often difficult to separate from reality (2014). In therapeutic terms, this condition is called "dissociation," where retraumatization feels like the event is happening again. Every gun violence incident, whether a survivor hears about it in the media, learns about it from someone, or is unfortunate to hear gunfire, reignites the lasting effects of triggers and retraumatization.

Although most gun homicide has been associated with urban neighbourhoods in Toronto, in recent times, affluent areas also experience these afflictions. Experiences of gun violence, injury, death, and other occurrences evoke mass levels of psychological trauma, affecting people and communities for lifetimes, with multi-generational consequences.

Despite frequent gun violence incidences and living in the shadow of daily fear, families and communities are ill-equipped to deal with the massive levels of trauma associated with gun violence. Limited resources with inadequate post-care services leave individuals, families, and communities in the lurch to deal with a lifetime of the intermittent resurgence of trauma.

Children and youth residing in disadvantaged communities with repetitive gun trauma, are expected to contribute to society as regular adult citizens when they grow older. Many of them are psychologically overburdened by traumatic loss and PTSD, without having processed their underlying trauma effectively.

This huge gap in adequate services, particularly post-care for trauma victims and survivors, continues to be an urgent need in communities inundated by gun violence. Responding to crisis and working with survivors of gun-related trauma, makes it easy to rank this type of trauma among the *'invisible wounds'* which demoralize human dignity. Without a well-constructed, holistic approach to gun violence trauma, families and communities will continue to suffer.

Traumatized people and communities experience incomprehensible anxiety and despair on every level of existence. Holistically, the effects of trauma are inter-generational, reverberating on the physical, emotional, intellectual, behavioural, spiritual, and socio-economical levels. This colossal problem needs to be viewed with the intent to treat it as the epidemic it is, utilizing best practices, cultural sensitivity, and trauma-informed practices.

CHAPTER 10

COMMUNITY AND INVISIBLE WOUNDS

"In every community, there is work to be done. In every nation, there are wounds to heal. In every heart, there is the power to do it."
- **Marianne Williamson**

COMMUNITY VIOLENCE HAPPENS SUDDENLY AND without warning. Community trauma begins at the onset of these distressing events, resulting in a trail of *'wounds'* which lasts throughout one's lifetime. These wounds are intertwined with the collective, as individuals and families experience tremendous loss. They become submerged within the framework of the community.

Research repeatedly attests that an enduring historical connection has been established between community trauma and the ongoing social inequities plaguing some social groups. Imperilled by repetitive gun violence trauma, underserved communities live with the persistent stigma of racism, oppression, and social inequities.

Gun violence deaths are intentional homicides. Aside from the atrocity that mystifies the mind, these crimes have ripple effects beyond the original loss of human life. They blight the lives of the victim's family and the community, who are forever being labelled as "secondary victims" (UNODC, 2019), and create violent environments that negatively impact society, the economy, and government institutions.

The resultant psychological wounds from community trauma are a significant public health issue, affecting the health of peoples and families, not only in Toronto but across Canada and the world. The National Police Federation (NPF) reports an incremental rise in gun-related homicide, citing the sharp incline of handguns as the primary weapon used in the reported 261 deaths of 2019. The NPF further decry the 2020 "assault" or "assault-style" firearm ban, calling on the Canadian government to enact further safety measures.

> The NPF calls for the best use of legislative powers to effectively address crime reduction, gang diversion, safe communities, secure borders, Canadian enforcement agency integration, and cross-border safety of the public and all police officers.

This work concurs with the NPF's claim, that current safety measures and public health strategies to combat gun violence or constructive methods to adequately address the issue are inadequate.

Community violence has been globally defined as *"Exposure to intentional acts of interpersonal violence committed in public areas by individuals who are not intimately related to the victim."* Although the term includes a host of other violent acts, this work focuses on gun violence, with the express intent to stress the significant public health problem cited by the World Health Organization and other global organizations.

Dating back to the early 1980s, scholars and researchers have identified the impending harm from exposure to, and the persistently sustained community violence that presently hounds our society. Working with victims and survivors of trauma afforded me a meticulously detailed view into the extensive mental, physical, emotional, intellectual, psycho-social, and spiritual impairments of those aggrieved by gun violence trauma.

Internal and external symptoms of gun violence, possess far-reaching and long-lasting effects that will continue to plague victims and survivors for the rest of their lives.

Starting at the low end of the spectrum, people exposed to psychological harm, can be adversely affected and develop arousals in the following areas: information about a death in the media or word of mouth; many are petrified at hearing the sound/s of an active firearm engagement; witnessing an incident; familiar with a person or family affected by gun violence; and much more significantly, being a victim or survivor of this formidable adversary.

Exposure to unremitting, insistent community violence, represents a unique form of trauma with psychological symptoms which researchers continue to unearth.

Hypervigilance ranks high on the graduated table, particularly in urban communities. Youth function from the perspective that 'it' could happen at any time and that 'it' might happen to them, their friends, or their loved ones. Hypervigilance is a state of continuous alertness, where a person expects what they fear the most to occur at any moment. During a hypervigilant state, arousal increases with high responsiveness to stimuli, and a constant scanning of the environment for imminent threats.

I worked with an 8-year-old who regularly hid in a closet, with body tremors and hands over his ears as he relived the agony of hearing gunfire. His older cousin was killed at point-blank range when he answered a knock on his apartment door. Unfortunately, this 8-year-old was present with other relatives.

At such close range, one would assume that the sound is indeed deafening. But much more extreme is the pandemonium that follows with screaming, shockwaves, hysteria, and the continuous presence of police, blaring sirens, paramedics, responders, and seeing his cousin's body being wheeled away in a body bag. After three months of continually barricading himself in that closet, his family doctor diagnosed him with acute stress disorder (ASD), followed by a later diagnosis of post-traumatic stress disorder (PTSD).

A PTSD diagnosis is given even if someone has only one of the following experiences:
   a   Directly experienced a traumatic event
   b) Witnessed, in person, the traumatic event occurring to someone or others
   c) Learned that someone close to you experienced. or was threatened by a traumatic event, or
   d) Repeatedly exposed to graphic details of traumatic events

Regrettably, this young boy experienced all those symptoms and lived in a community where 'it' continues. He will more than likely encounter other incidents. Anyone experiencing such a traumatic event undergoes much more than emotional wounds. Although the odd person might be mildly affected, which is rare, an assortment of impending psychological effects is imminent.

PTSD is most closely associated with gun violence and is defined as:

"A mental health condition that's triggered by witnessing or experiencing terrifying events, such as a natural disaster, serious accident, sexual assault, rape, or threat of death."

Associated symptoms include severe anxiety, flashbacks, nightmares, yearnings, and uncontrollable thoughts about the event. Hearing of, witnessing, or experiencing gun violence induces PTSD. Among the stresses related to such an incident are the accumulative symptoms of headaches, depression, insomnia, mistrust, fear, and loss of safety, to list a few. When someone has been injured and survived, this person must automatically be grouped with folks who have suffered psychological trauma associated with war or even catastrophic disasters.

May 2013 saw a significant change when the DSM-4 categorized PTSD under "trauma and stressor-related disorders," reversing the previous diagnosis from 'anxiety disorder.'

Although fraught with emotional pain, Shakespeare's quote, *"the wounds invisible, that love's keen arrows make,"* cannot equate to the agonizing devastation that gun violence induces. The term *'invisible wounds'* has been increasingly associated with war and veterans dating back to the mid-nineteenth century.

An *'invisible wound'* is "a cognitive, emotional, or behavioural condition that can be associated with trauma or serious adverse life events."

While hospitalized survivors are released and deemed to be "recovered," the injury and wounds gun violence survivors sustain exceed the mundane, and must be categorized as psychological trauma. In my years of working with primary gun violence trauma and providing post-care to survivors, I have yet to encounter survivors who considered their encounter superficial or casual, and weren't petrified after gun violence trauma.

Trauma survivors are known to be living with this *'invisible wound,'* always unnoticed, despite functioning in a chaotic state, except for manifestations of behavioural patterns, or periods of symptomatic physical reactions. While prolonged exposure to trauma has been known to hinder human progress, gun violence's *'invisible wounds'* can be traced through a psychological lens on specific areas of functioning.

A survivor's sense of safety and security, which is the building block for all other human aspirations, becomes non-existent in the immediate aftermath of gun violence trauma.

Researchers have identified multiple phases in which particular emotions, behaviours, and other reactions are fairly typical of traumatic reactions (Alexander & Klein, 2005; Freedy & Simpson, 2007; Goldman & Galea, 2014). Due to the uniqueness of traumatic grief reactions, some would vary depending on the characteristics, personality, and grieving style of the victim or survivor. Early intervention on a holistic level can minimize extreme effects and assist in promoting healing and resilience.

1. **Acute Phase:** has been categorized at the onset of trauma with displays of initial shock, denial, disbelief, and in some cases, fainting spells. Critical incident stress debriefing (CISD) is done during this phase with Psychological First Aid.
2. **Intermediate Phase:** is characterized by feelings of fear, anxiety, retaliatory attacks (particularly among youth), depression, insomnia, attention deficit, and transitory panic attacks, to name a few.
3. **Long-Term Phase:** has been named the *'coming to terms with reality phase,'* where acceptance is looming on the horizon, where adjustments are slowly being made, and the potential for relapse is still exceptionally high. During this critical stage, unhealthy and untreated health behaviours are usually cemented into illnesses, warranting specialized therapeutic

services. Those who have developed unhealthy coping habits such as substance abuse, sexual promiscuity, social isolation, or withdrawal, would enter the long, arduous journey of relearning new coping skills and making tough choices for health recovery.

Physical Reactions

Psychological supports from the onset of trauma and mainly during the early phase of active trauma, significantly assist in normalizing the trauma and promoting steps to resilience for victims, survivors, the wider community, and crisis responders, who are also involuntarily affected.

Hypervigilance, with other behavioural reactions, is activated on all levels of functioning. A heightened awareness of the imminent threat is real to survivors. In the early stages after an incident—the first 48 hours—many survivors will not leave their homes and need constant reassurance. They will not walk alone, or even answer their doors if they haven't been notified or expecting someone to visit.

One survivor disclosed how she frequently froze to a standstill whenever the doorbell rang, or if there was a knock on the door, immediately thinking that someone intended to harm her. Her breathing became laboured; her heart rate increased dramatically, and she felt as though her heart was jumping out of her chest. She experienced uncontrollable tremors and couldn't speak until the imaginary threat was nullified, which took 15 to 60 minutes. During a weekly session, she recounted when an old friend decided to visit without informing her.

Although she was sitting, her stiffened body indicated how terrified she was. Her eyes were bulging, and ready tears welled and streamed down her face. Her breathing became laboured to the point of hyperventilation. It took quite a few minutes to get this client relaxed enough to continue our session. As part of her week's assignment, using 'active coping strategies,' she was encouraged to advise family and friends of her experiences, the reactions she continues to have, and request that people notify her before visiting.

Psychological debriefing within 48 to 72 hours is beneficial to reduce such impending suffering for victims, survivors, and witnesses of active gun violence trauma. These debriefs should be conducted by a trained facilitator, versed in critical incident stress debriefing (CISD), who can empathize with and encourage witnesses, victims, and survivors, through those techniques, to minimize and help alleviate immediate and long-term anxieties.

CISD is not only critical and therapeutic for crisis responders but extremely important for victims, survivors, and witnesses of gun violence trauma as well. Not restricted to victims, survivors, and witnesses, the wider community is also adversely impacted by any traumatic violence where it occurs. Debriefing should also be offered to the broader community affected by gun violence, which negatively affects the community's equilibrium.

Constructively, immediate responses to trauma can reduce some adverse physical reactions such as persistent fatigue, sleep disorders, nightmares, fear of reoccurrence, anxiety focused on flashbacks, depression, and avoidance of emotions, sensations, or activities that are even remotely associated with the trauma.

A child's reaction might include other symptoms such as chills or sweating, stomach aches with gastrointestinal changes, diarrhea, dizziness, grinding teeth, or fainting spells.

Although children exhibit extraordinary resilience in many circumstances, research has shown that a person's ethnicity, gender, psycho-social support, and social-economic status can gravely impact their ability to bounce back from severe trauma such as gun violence. Lower-income household's exposure to ongoing stressors and continuous traumatic events, were found to correlate with physical ailments and other depressive symptoms (Nandi et al., 2009).

Emotional Reactions

Depression is an emotionally weakening illness, which impacts humans on the physical and psychological levels. Many have expressed, how they struggle with the swampy reactions of sadness, despair and hopelessness that often threaten their very survival. Clients have reported the desperate need for air as they worked with what feels like "life being sucked out of them."

Depression is described as *"a common medical illness that negatively affects how you feel, the way you think, and how you act."*

Many descriptions fail to explore the type of depression associated with gun violence trauma. Closely associated with anxiety, depression is the most common psychiatric complaint. Those who suffer from anxiety also complain of depression, which functions in tandem with anxiety. Many definitions of depression provide a lightly descriptive analysis, with the added statement that depression can be cured. Such descriptions do not consider gun violence trauma.

The level of suicidal ideologies among mothers tormented with gun violence trauma is astronomical. I have responded to calls between 1 and 3 a.m. where mothers have reached out in desperation. Some were in the act of committing suicide, and others were at the scene where they envisioned committing suicide.

These extreme reactions occur in the 'intermediary phase' of trauma, where reality begins to sink in, where the death of a loved one is verified. Generally, this threat formulates after the funeral and burial have occurred, and life beckons a return to a type of normalcy that society requires. Whereas survivors' mentality is silently screaming with wishes for time and all clocks to stand still, the world continues to plod steadily along with a 'business-as-usual' expectation.

Retraumatization rears its tormenting head during the 'long-term phase,' blending anger, fears, sadness, desire for revenge, numbness, and a host of other painful emotions into the proverbial *"tangled ball of grief"* that's often used to educate and raise awareness. During this phase, employers expect workers to return to their jobs and function at full capacity; teachers are looking to youth and younger students, questioning their productivity; friends and extended family cannot understand the reserved approaches and behaviours that a survivor displays.

Increasing demands for a survivor to function "the same as before…" becomes a tipping point, especially for mothers who attempted to return to work, despite cautious instructions to pay close attention to negative, intrusive thoughts. Many survivors desire to "return to normal," but normal is now relative to where they are on their grief/trauma journey, and the level of trauma they have experienced. Those who experience complicated grief will have the deluxe combination of emotions, including retraumatization—a resurfacing of packed emotional pain related to previous traumas.

Cognitive Reactions

"My mind is staging a war against me." This disclosure from a mother struggling to cope with a recent gun violence death paved the way for others to chime in during a research study with a small grant from Women's College Hospital in Toronto. To further enhance our already established system of care, Out Of Bounds aspired to develop and implement a community-based peer mutual support group, where survivor-mothers would

engage in critical dialogue about the development, structure and processes, designed to meet their specific grief and trauma needs.

During that year's process, mothers divulged the confusion and disorientation they felt over simple acts like brushing their teeth in the morning. Many convulsed and laughed at themselves and each other, as they recalled how they "forgot" what they went to the bathroom to do. Some forgot how to spell their names or remember simple things like moving from one room to the next for "something," but couldn't think what it was.

Among the various effects of traumatic loss, short-term memory is one of the cognitive effects which hampers a "return to normal" for survivors, especially students. Truancy becomes delinquent behaviour for those with symptoms of poor concentration, insomnia, and short-term memory loss.

Survivors spontaneously create imagery to process their grief and better understand what their loved one might have suffered in the last few minutes of their life. Repetitive flashbacks of that imagery, which might not be the actual event, become an established disruption, requiring various therapeutic interventions, like re-storying, to gradually replace the imagery. Hypervigilance bounces around and often takes centre stage, hijacking survivors' desire to progress, or in some cases, contributing to the isolation and withdrawal which some crave.

Laughter during traumatic recounting is recognized as medicinal for healing. Grief-healing requires a self-motivated approach, utilizing every human emotion in a blended modality of reflection, crying and yes, laughter. Humour is specifically effective, especially when we can laugh at ourselves. The Good Book reminds us that "A cheerful heart is good medicine."

Behavioural Reactions

Depending on the proximity, the severity of a traumatic incident, if a death results or an imminent threat exists, immediate behaviours such as screaming, fainting, shock reactions and weeping are initial behaviour reactions.

Behaviours following a shooting, affect people on various levels. Immediate family and eyewitnesses react differently, but behavioural reactions tell the distinctive story of how intense the trauma affects those directly involved. One group member reported how she self-soothed with alcohol "as though the liquor store belonged to her." Another expressed how petrified she felt about the location where her son was killed. Although she lived approximately five minutes from the area, she would detour 25 minutes to avoid it.

Youth behaviour changes drastically. Some good students who deliberately engaged in truancy became aggressive and utterly rebellious against anyone in authority. Others felt that living and functioning didn't matter since their sibling or friend died, while others avoided any discussions on the matter, behaving as though it never happened. A dichotomy sometimes develops between increased appetite and loss of appetite; weight gain and weight loss, depending on the person and situation.

Other deeply concerning areas for youth are the dangerous behaviours and combined unhealthy traits that they participate in. WHO identified bullying, substance abuse, sexual violence, and misbehaviour among both sexes in their 2020 violence report:

> Youth homicide and non-fatal violence not only contribute greatly to the global burden of premature death, injury, and disability but also have a serious, often lifelong, impact on a person's psychological and social functioning. This can affect victims' families, friends,

and communities. Youth violence increases the costs of health, welfare, and criminal justice services; reduces productivity; decreases the value of property.

Timeframe varies with grief's uniqueness, but whether people learned about a shooting, were survivors, or belonged to the broader community, behavioural reactions evoked different mannerisms. Insomnia is a common side effect for most survivors, which precipitated other unwholesome behaviour patterns, such as inability to concentrate, distractedness, listlessness, lethargy, and disinterest in self-care, among other mannerisms.

Spiritual Reactions

Spirituality derives from our connection with the spiritual aspect of ourselves. As humans, we are created with an innate desire to recognize and become attuned with the various parts of how we function, including recognition of a 'Higher Power.' Most scholars estimate that there are around 4,200 active religions globally, with 12 listed as the most frequently practiced and having the most followers.

Spirituality is a universal experience where human beings connect with the "God-Being" they recognize as higher than themselves. Devoutness is found and expressed through a personal relationship with God or a Higher Power, while engaging in some form of worship through prayers, scriptural texts, singing, or gathering with others. Many describe their spirituality as sacred, transcendent, profoundly calming, through interconnectedness with the divine.

As an expression of that connection and faith, people are typically drawn to churches, temples, mosques, or synagogues. Some worship in nature under the canopy of the heavens, finding solace and inner strength from being outdoors, while others seek solitude, practicing actions that turn inward to connect with their higher self. When life is tranquil and without emotional turmoil, human beings are at peace with their "Higher Power," enjoying a peaceful co-existence.

However, when trouble strikes, there is a tendency for many to lose the very faith they found comforting and transcending. Many question the God who has the ability, the God with all power, who chose not to save their child. In my role as minister, I've officiated many gun-related funerals and burials and worked with many who professed faith in God but struggled under the enormity of traumatic pain. I've been grilled on the topic of why God would allow something so dreadful to happen to youth not engaged in criminal activities.

Mothers and families have lost their professed faith because the suffering was too intense to endure. One mother who professed strong faith and went to church religiously stopped going to church after she buried her son because she felt God turned His back on her.

She resorted to substance abuse to numb her pain. She distanced herself from friends and family in that circle of churchgoers. She felt that she could escape the pain for a few hours as she slept but had to keep drinking when she awoke as reality sank in. This pattern of unhealthy coping continued for close to a year until reason, grief's process, and residual faith rekindled the embers of her faith. She stopped drinking as abruptly as she began and engaged in healing.

Deserved Acknowledgement

"Grief is a most peculiar thing; we're so helpless in the face of it. It's like a window that will simply open of its own accord. The room grows cold, and we can do nothing but shiver. But it opens a little less each time, and a little less; and one day we wonder what has become of the [intensity] of it."
- Arthur Golden, (Adapted, Rev. Sky Starr, 2010)

GRIEVERS' BEATITUDES

Blessed are the grievers who, though unprepared, step out on the road of pain and loss.

Blessed are the grievers who are not afraid to whimper, moan and wallow, during the intensity of their loss.

Blessed are the grievers who embrace the harsh lessons that the 'grim reaper' Grief teaches.

Blessed are the grievers whose hearts and minds seek to learn and understand *how* grief, loss, and trauma affect their lives.

Blessed are the grievers who know that they are the experts of their own grief processes.

Blessed are the grievers who face each day with heads held high despite the deep yearnings inside.

Blessed are the grievers who understand that grief cannot be hurried but endured, and accepted, until transformation and connection are made with the "soul" part of self.

Fractured Communities

Blessed are the grievers who find ways to cope when unexpected triggers erupt.

Blessed are the grievers who desperately seek to put words to their emotions.

Blessed are the grievers who often struggle in isolation and silence.

Blessed are the grievers who identify their needs and find the courage to express them.

Blessed are the grievers whose hearts, minds, and spirits are transformed through trauma.

Blessed are the grievers who emerge with a new purpose through *'meaning-making.'*

Blessed are the grievers who can tell their stories and listen to someone else's.

Blessed are the grievers who gain empowerment and resilience with time and courage.

Blessed are the grievers who can smile or laugh through their tears.

Blessed are the grievers who learn to live again and find joy within their communities.

Blessed are the grievers who, despite their daily struggles, extend a helping hand to a **'freshman griever.'**

Blessed are the grievers who learn and practice the art of *'personal self-care.'*

Blessed are the grievers who can extend *'the art of comforting'* and listening to others.

Blessed are the grievers who understand that grieving is a lifelong journey.

© **Rev. Sky Starr, April 2010**

Spirituality

> *"Learn your theories well, but put them aside when you touch the miracle of the living soul. Not theories alone, but your own creative individuality must decide."*
> **- Carl Jung**

As a therapist, I'm trained in and became clinically acquainted with the various concepts of therapeutic practices. Undeniably, acquiring theoretical and experiential knowledge is critical to understanding how to journey with those who are grieving. Yet, the field of psychology makes it challenging to marry spirituality with therapeutic practices. Models of care and language such as diagnosis, treatments, pathology, and disorders, steer clear of the core self, "the soul," which is precisely where grievers feel the strongest sense of anguish, abandonment, and deep sorrow.

We often glibly use the word *"holistic"* but fail to explore all its nuances when we as human beings feel wounded, betrayed, vulnerable, or are in anguished pain. That inner part of ourselves—the soul—often remains obscured. Carl Jung understood that the *"soul"* part of humanity is that area where only the divine can touch, massage, and eventually induce healing. Plato's theory of the soul named it the *"psyche."* Drawing from his teacher Socrates, he theorized that the soul is the "essence of a person, which fueled behaviour," believing it to be the "incorporeal, eternal occupant of our being."

At the onset of trauma, many plead and tearfully negotiate with God or their Higher Power as they try to deal with the emptiness and meaninglessness of loss. Listed as part of the grief stages, *'bargaining'* remains a desperate option for those overly apprehensive when faced with the brusqueness of gun violence death. Many expressed how they begin to doubt this "so-called Higher Power who couldn't save their child." Cynicism, apathy, and mistrust overshadow the faith expressed, when life flowed peacefully and steadily like an uninterrupted stream.

The proverbial question, *"Why?"* is always asked, especially to a minister who most people feel would have a ready answer. I don't know of any minister or person who has a satisfying answer. There is no answer. Any words that might be expressed are neither adequate nor plausible.

My modest response remains the same after close to 20 years of working in the trenches of fresh trauma, witnessing humanity at its most vulnerable, and understanding the desolating burrows of a future dwarfed by trauma. If your God is all-powerful, then your God can answer, *"why?"*

The omnipotent, yet compassionate God I know, understands that the human heart crumbles under the weight of sorrow and excruciating pain; He is described in Isaiah 53:3 as *"...a Man of sorrows and acquainted with grief."* I believe that God is big enough to be with each grieving heart that walks *"through the valley and the shadow of death"* (Psalm 23:4a).

I further remind querying minds that Jesus, in suffering and facing death, also asked *"why?"* so they are not alone in their desire to better understand the abyss of torment into which they're suddenly plunged. Consistency is the only evidence of abiding faith. Human companionship does not merely have a physical presence. It's retaining the assurance that you can rely on another person for sincere friendship, be available to talk, listen, reason, and be an accountability partner for the duration of the grief journey.

The Roman orator, Marcus Tullius Cicero, penned the endearing words, *"Friendship improves happiness and abates misery, by the doubling of our joy and the dividing of our grief."* So too, those who accompany us on grief's journey become *'grief-dividers'* who lighten the burdensome task demanded by grief with reassuring camaraderie.

Protracted Journey

Despite our most sincere intentions to speed up the process, each person must endure the lengthy path of grief. Grieving is a slow, laborious progression that helps us tune in to our inner selves—the soul part of ourselves—where we learn valuable, dormant lessons that help us evolve. These "soul lessons" contribute to the necessary adaptation, which thrust us into becoming wiser, more compassionate beings. Much like the process of metamorphosis, we eventually understand and embrace that grieving is a necessary part of life, an eventuality that we must all experience.

Grief has no timeline. It cannot, no, will not be rushed or coerced. It's a unique, individual process. It's viability is for every human being with a tenacity to teach, renew, and rouse dormant souls. Whether we balk or resist defiantly, once the process has started, there is no retreating.

Unfortunately, as humans, we learn our best lessons through pain. The process of a painful experience leaves an ingrained imprint on our psyche, which resurfaces as dynamic memory when needed. These *'life lessons'* help us attune to the deeper part of ourselves, where our souls, with advanced knowledge, assist with revised identities.

The phenomenon of the soul continues to baffle humanity. In our frustrations, we try to reframe the knowledge from our inner selves. Clients often state, "A little voice inside of me told me…." Our internal voice provides direction and intuitive 'knowing' which guides our decision-making, daily choices, and future plans. That same inner compass advises us during painful lessons, gently nudging and occasionally plummeting us through fiery furnaces where growth is not an option.

It is affirming and stimulating to find attestation from Dr. Alan Woldelt, one of North America's leading death and grief counsellors, acknowledging that "grief is a soul-based journey." He expressly lists Carl Jung among the esteemed writers he reads and credits Jung's writings which helped him understand:

> That every psychological struggle is ultimately a matter of spirituality. In the end, as we human beings mourn, we must discover meaning to go on living our tomorrows without the physical presence of someone we loved. Death and grief are spiritual journeys of the heart and soul.

Crisis of Faith

Case:

Initially, all I heard were deep, mournful sounds of weeping. I knew that whoever was calling got choked up in the process and needed a moment or two to collect themself. I repeated my name in between pauses and articulated that I'd remain on the line until the person was composed enough to speak. After more sniffles and heavy breathing, an emotional voice stated she needed my services as a minister to officiate at her daughter's funeral but angrily exclaimed, "I don't want any mention of God!"

Community and Invisible Wounds

I paused, took a deep breath and calmly reminded her that she called me as a minister and even addressed me as Rev. Sky. She explained that she wanted me to do the funeral for her daughter being a female minister, and because of what I do in the community.

I calmly replied that I'd be happy to officiate but would need more information via an appointment. The person was in the parking lot of my office. I just wrapped up with another client and had a half-hour window until my next appointment.

As she sat wringing her hands in bewilderment, this mother was also seething with rage. I realized then that I had seen her before. She was acquainted with the work we do with gun violence victims and survivors. However, her crisis of faith conflicted with her insistence that she needed a minister, specifically a minister associated with gun violence trauma, to do the funeral.

With a steady gaze and gentle yet firm demeanour, I advised this mother that youth attending the funeral between the ages of 15 and 19 and upwards would need encouragement and hope. I also reminded her that the funeral was not only for her and the immediate family, but that these youth would be anticipating expressions to help soothe the immeasurable pain, confusion, and even retaliatory emotions they were experiencing.

I suggested that we could use other names such as Divine Providence or Higher Power as substitutes. I also advised her that I'll be wearing my clerical collar, making it easier for youth and others to approach me if needed. After much deliberating, she agreed.

More than 400 youth attended that funeral and clung to every word said, while some participated in 'open floor' speeches. Many approached me later to express gratitude and ask poignant questions. I spent an extra 45 minutes talking to them and trying to alleviate their anxieties and fears.

An interesting surprise was meeting a minister who introduced himself as the pastor at the church where that mother and family attended. Mom refused to have the funeral at the church. Her crisis of faith included shunning the pastor who, in her eyes, sided with God and didn't pray hard enough to save her daughter.

The fascinating part is that she not only listened with rapt attention during the ceremony, but that she held my gaze whenever I looked her way. Hopeful encouragement was vital to her as well, even if her speech and actions indicated otherwise. At the height of such a crisis of faith, she, like many others, lash out at God, Higher Power, Divine Providence, or whatever name they choose to use, who they feel disappointed them. Yet, the contradiction also depicts the human spirit's conflict, and the anguish associated with suffering such sudden and intense trauma.

John of the Cross penned, '*The Dark Night of the Soul,*' which many parallel as a poetic signpost for suffering or relative to human trials, when it wasn't initially intended as such. Yet, the phrase is continually expressed in polarity with a crisis of faith and spiritual struggles related to emotional trauma.

Over the years, mothers have increasingly expressed anger at God or their Higher Power, with a lengthy period of denying their faith, replacing it with liquor, drugs, or other unhealthy activities, intending to numb or minimize the pain they're experiencing. Group sessions, research, and in-house data all point to the perplexity of human emotions and the shattering blow the psyche receives with trauma such as gun violence.

In an article entitled '*Mother Teresa's Crisis of Faith,*' Time Magazine divulged the continuous struggle the notable figure, Mother Teresa, had with suffering, and the crisis of faith she endured during most of her ministry. Her crisis surrounded the inability to sense God's presence. The author chronicled Mother Teresa's many letters, who later requested that they be removed from her file, but was denied. The article revealed that:

> In more than 40 communications, many of which have never before been published, she bemoans the dryness, darkness, loneliness, and "torture she is undergoing." "The smile," she writes, "is a mask or 'a cloak that covers everything.'"

Many mothers can identify with Mother Teresa, and of course, the admission of her faith crisis can encourage them. Witnessing or experiencing suffering exposes our own vulnerability.

Congruently, mothers and others have experienced the most gruesome sudden deaths and strongly affirm that their faith in God, in their specific Higher Power, maintained their sanity. Many felt that divine strength through prayers, alignment with the church community, and spiritual practices aided them to better cope and heal. These mothers attest that faith in God or their Higher Power and the assurance of that solid, spiritual background promoted their healing, shifted them towards meaning-making, and enhanced their resilience (Bailey et al., 2015).

Spontaneously at our group sessions, mothers suggests and requests prayer before beginning and at the conclusion. Our mutual peer sessions adopt actions and practices through consensus. Despite their insistence that they were no longer interested in or believed in God, they too agreed to include a spiritual component in the groups' activities.

Mothers who maintained their faith showed consistent signs of healing, with progressive steps towards empowerment and resilience. Yet, their journey was also fraught with erratic triggers and trauma S.T.U.G.S like the other mothers. The noticeable difference was their ability to navigate the processes with stronger resolution and confidence in a divine, invisible strength that supported them.

Faith and reliance on a Higher Power contribute significantly to the traumatic healing processes. In conformity with trauma's tasks, individual faith provides the courage and endurance to "turn inward, slow down, embrace the pain," and allow the supportive strategies and atmosphere to assist in promoting healing.

Many who relied on their faith expressed how they spent more time in prayer, reading, discussions with faith leaders, and other spiritual exercises. Although they often buckled under the strain and pushed themselves, their appetite improved, and insomnia gradually dwindled. These intentional activities contributed to holistic recovery, although trauma remained a permanent part of their lives.

Not only does spirituality enhance the grieving process, but faith, in combination with strategic supports, is critical for traumatic healing. Only God, a Higher Power or Divine Providence, can provide the inner strength for survivors to endure the intense, psychological pain that gun violence survivors must endure.

Healing to attain a level of functioning capacity, requires extremely hard work. Therapists, counsellors, facilitators, and well-wishers can support, encourage, and journey alongside. However, I believe the task of grieving, reconciling emotions, and arriving at acceptance towards empowerment and resilience, can only be achieved with divine help.

As a therapist, I can distinguish some specific areas within my scope of capabilities. I am a trained and experienced professional, culturally competent, empathetic, encouraging, committed, and supportive. But can I provide hope, instill resilience, or build faith? No. Only the divine can instill hope; only the divine can give the inner resolve while providing those critical elements with grievers' willingness, making Carl Jung's words quite fitting. *"Embrace your grief, for there your soul will grow."*

Unfortunately, survivors not attuned with some level of spirituality often find themselves "stuck in grief" for extended periods.

One case stands out. Although this mother grew up in a "religious environment," as she termed it, she confessed that she never "latched on to that part of her upbringing." She readily admitted that she had no faith in any kind of Higher Power, although she wanted her son to have all the religious rites at his funeral. There were numerous instances when she openly expressed, "Today is a really bad day, and I'm leaning on the faith that you have to carry me through." What I provided was encouragement.

We can inspire, motivate, and even stimulate, but no one can instill hope in another. One definition of hope is *"a feeling of trust."* That feeling of trust in someone or something "bigger than ourselves" can only be attained through personal, spiritual awareness.

In addition, various physical ailments compound their journey. The holistic path to healing must encircle all the areas that include our humanness—mind, soul, body, and spirit. Therapists, counsellors, facilitators, and empathizers must provide care on a holistic basis to yield maximum healing, empowerment, meaning-making, and resilience. Spirituality or religion works in tandem with meaning-making, and needs to be a critical component of the growth and wellness process during trauma, regardless of the client's faith affiliation.

CHAPTER 11

HONOURING OUR GRIEF

"Deep grief sometimes is almost like a specific location, a coordinate on a map of time. When you are standing in that forest of sorrow, you cannot imagine that you could ever find your way to a better place. But if someone can assure you that they themselves have stood in that same place, and now have moved on, sometimes this will bring hope."
- Elizabeth Gilbert

GRIEF, LOSS, TRAUMA, AND MOURNING share a unique camaraderie but are classified as dreaded foes to human beings. No one is ever really prepared for either of these situations. In fact, none of us want to encounter or deal with them. Generally, the topic is never discussed until death happens in our family or within our circles.

Fractured Communities

Responding to crises and working with several victims and survivors, I feel very strongly that we should be somewhat prepared for the foreseeable. Death is a certainty which, as I've noticed over the years, people are ill-prepared to deal with, while others go to great lengths to stifle their grieving process. In reality, everyone knows that death will someday come knocking at their door, without exceptions.

Grief and mourning must be honoured. This mourning period is ushered in with the drastic severing of emotional ties with a loved one in our nuclear family, close relatives, or someone close to us. The depth of pain is dependent on the level of intimacy or closeness we develop with that person.

"You didn't know that pain had a voice, far less able to speak?" Pain speaks, and if we're open enough, we might be able to hear that inner voice respond to your amazement and have a meaningful dialogue. Seriously though, speaking to pain is similar to self-talk. We honour our grief—the sadness, deep hurt, the emotional distress we're feeling—by acknowledging, expressing, and allowing those feelings, the pain, to speak, both inwardly and outwardly.

Pain's language manifests through the anguish which follows a sudden death. Pain's language can be gleaned from the moans and groans of the broken heart striving to be voiced. Pain's language is often heard in the community's collective voices drowning in traumatic grief; pain's language is definitely heard in the audible cries from a fresh or latent griever, who finally understands that giving pain this noticeable platform is necessary and appropriate.

Grief's entrance into any life is often unwelcomed, unorthodox, and in most cases dramatic. Known as "The Unwelcomed Intruder," Grief takes up permanent residence wherever it enters. Grief remains an unwanted guest despite attempts at dismissal, shunning, and resistance, using incessant nudges and painful prodding as Grief seeks to attract the griever's attention. This *'meddler'* never tires of jabbing the elbow and shifting the pain pendulum until Grief does "Grief's Work" of painful reorganizing priorities, rearranging areas that need reassessing, and reconstructing a directional purpose from pain to renewal.

"Grief's Work" raises the griever's conscious awareness of the progressive efforts of adaptation in all areas of functioning.

After the initial shock and disbelief, the fresh griever is expected to lean towards adaptation of the grieving stages (Strobe, 2015). This adaptation stage is a realization that a death has occurred, and that the grieving process has started. During this *'adaptation stage,'* the person at the entrance of the "Grief Tunnel," now identified as a *Freshman griever,* needs to allow Grief to initiate "Grief's Work." This person is expected to mentally and emotionally begin to disengage from the lost person. Although the physical ties to the person who died have been irrevocably severed, the other phases are usually challenging.

Here's where Kubler Ross' stages of grief indicate sensibility. Non-academics—the everyday layperson—tend to understand the simple stages much better than adaptation. Every *"Freshman griever"* is not only reluctant to embark on this 'Grief Work' process, but for many survivors who are in shock, denial, and disbelief, the havoc around them is still an unbelievably bad dream from which they're hoping they'll wake up. The idea of adaptation is not even a thought at this stage.

Case:

During a customary viewing on the evening before the funeral I was to officiate, the mother and I stood before the casket where her son's body was prepped for folks to pay their final respects. She suddenly turned to me and asked if I thought it was possible that her son was in a coma and that the funeral directors were not aware of it yet. Reverting to my nurses' training and gathering every other experience I had, I made sure my body touched hers as I calmly but firmly responded.

I asked her to place her forefinger in front of his nostrils and tell me if she felt any warm breath. 'Nothing,' was her response. I then asked if she thought his chest would be rising and falling if he was still breathing. To which she nodded. To my next question, "Do you still think he might be in a coma?" She didn't respond. All I could do then was squeeze her hand to affirm my presence and support. Even then, she had difficulty accepting her son's death.

From learning of the death up to this time, we participated in two weeks of meetings with city officials, funeral directors and making burial arrangements. Granted, she had not seen her son's body until it was released to the funeral home. She mentioned that he was always home on time, didn't run around with friends a lot. She referred to him as "a homebody." Even with the apparent evidence that he hadn't been coming home or sleeping in his bed, none of it seemed to register. She still hoped she would "wake up from this dream-like circumstance around her."

Usually, after the burial and lowering of the casket into the ground, survivor-mothers tentatively allow the realization of finality to be a possibility. Some slowly begin to accept the thought of life's termination but still struggle to say the word, 'dead.' Even at the ten-year life marker, many continue to use the phrase, "I lost my son to gun violence."

One mother felt the need to talk to her son and made a minimum of nine trips to the cemetery daily to do so, even though she had to drive more than half an hour each way. She disclosed that she remembered something she forgot to say to him each time she returned home and went back to talk more. She admitted that she felt closer to him there. Many years later, she refuses to go close to the area, which evokes severe inceptions of panic attack reactions.

Until the griever begins to accept that the person has died and gives pain the recognition, with the emotional outlet of experiencing the pain, Grief's Work cannot commence. Acknowledging the woundedness of spirit and the heart's brokenness are signposts that one is ready to co-create with Grief. By yielding to the pain and acknowledging a death—even though one might be far from acceptance—the initiation of "Grief Work" receives the psychological green light to begin.

Allowing pain to fully express itself, whether, through crying, wallowing and emotional reasoning, the griever indicates a willingness to participate as Grief begins the journey of healing. There will, of course, be the usual 'start-and-stop,' relapses and resuming periods, especially in the first six months to a year, but the Grim Tutor is non-judgemental. He continues to nudge, jostle, and push the pain pendulum until it arrives at a steady momentum.

Grief's companionship is a lifelong process. Any loss we experience diminishes in intensity related to the initial pain. Still, the grief twinges will always remain as we remember and reflect on the memories of that loved one.

Our lives will incorporate a series of losses along the way, but it will also be filled with ample periods of joyful, celebratory moments, a balanced tapestry of a meaningful life, a new type or *'normal'* if you will. Our old selves will be wiser, and hopefully, more compassionate, spiritually attuned, and understanding.

Extinguishing Closure

"There is no consciousness without pain. People will do anything, no matter how absurd, in order to avoid facing their own soul. One does not become enlightened by imagining figures of light, but by making the darkness conscious."
- Carl Jung

Fractured Communities

'Closure' is being used casually and even seriously in many instances, by relatives of the deceased; friends who are uncomfortable with another person's grief; well-meaning folks who are feeling sorry when someone is crying because they were triggered; the media, who don't always take into consideration the far-reaching influence they have; and especially by those who believe that life is and should always be pleasant, happy, void of death, grief, and suffering.

One of our best human characteristics is the inherent ability to retain information, to remember. As remembering beings, our memories help us store, recall, and retrieve life's incidents engraved on our cerebral imagery. Granted, some of those imagery will be painful, traumatic, and even unpleasant. Yet other memories of happiness, love and laughter assist in offsetting and harmonizing the pain with periods of joy; the trauma with bits of laughter; and the bitter emotions with happy memories.

During one of our group sessions, a survivor-mother was noticeably quiet. She was obviously brooding over a troublesome thought. We barely started our check-in when she angrily blurted out, "I wish people would stop asking me if I have closure yet. Who created that word anyway? I really hate that word!" She was approaching her son's death anniversary and was preparing for and anticipating the customary commemoration gathering. Emotions are usually high when approaching anniversary markers.

She recounted an interaction with a friend she attempted to discuss preparations for the second death anniversary gathering she was planning for her son. Her friend, who she felt would understand and would also know how important such an event was to her, blurted out, "It's been two years already. You haven't reached closure yet?"

Death anniversaries are simply remembering that that person lived and is now dead. Part of the healing process towards meaning-making is venerating a loved one's life.

We remember, honour, and celebrate the memory of that person. During planning, implementing, and observing the interactions, the mother and family members receive support, presence, and encouragement, as they continue to grieve the loss they sustained.

Other mothers instinctively encircled this freshly wounded mother, who, like many grievers, would experience "pangs of pain" as others act insensitively or express tactless words. Although her friend's comments wounded this mother, the underlying pain was that her friend didn't or couldn't identify with the loss that she experienced. Within this haven, she knew that those who travel similar roads understood; facilitators and this band of grief warriors identified this situation as one of the many unfeeling behaviours that grievers face.

Our session focused on the word "closure," which never fails to elevate blood pressures, including mine. We decided to identify the specific aspects of the frustrations and thoughts that it evoked. Mothers, a couple of fathers, and other grievers chimed in with the following:

1. My son's life mattered. I loved him, and I want to keep remembering him.
2. It's been only two years. Why am I expected to forget that he lived?
3. Hearing the word closure makes me feel like my child is just a thing, that he wasn't a person.
4. I don't think people realize how using the word closure hurts grieving people.
5. We need to make a petition to get this word removed from being associated with grief.
6. Friends should understand that because your child is dead, doesn't mean that his memory doesn't exist anymore.

7. There are times when I remember something funny about my daughter, and I feel like she's smiling and laughing with me. If closure really existed, I don't think I would feel that way.
8. How do we let people know how insensitive and degrading closure is and sounds?
9. Even though it's been five years since he died, I still feel his presence on special occasions. Closure doesn't exist.
10. When someone says that word to me, it makes me feel hopeless for a while.
11. I feel grateful that I can talk about my child without crying, but if closure really existed, it would mean that he's gone, forgotten, and we don't talk about him anymore. Just thinking about that makes me sad.
12. We should all agree to put out the sparks around closure like putting out a fire.

The consensus was that whenever anyone used *closure* to anyone, it was our duty to inform them that we had an extensive discussion on the ramifications of that word. By voting consensus, we had distinguished the word.

One group member suggested "burying" the word, and just for a fleeting moment, we entertained the idea, but someone else chimed in that if we were to do that, it would mean that we're giving *closure* an existence, which it doesn't have. This statement softened the moment with another fit of laughter, which brought the topic to a close. The group felt that we had successfully distinguished the term in our setting, although we would need to weigh every future encounter and gently educate where it's beneficial.

I, too, feel the tinge of annoyance whenever someone uses the word closure. It has become famed among politicians, media, and within cultural norms. During an interview with Global TV, I was asked if I think families who lost someone to gun violence would ever find closure. It was my distinct pleasure to respond without hesitation, "Absolutely not!" I was delighted to quote the mothers on national TV as saying, "There's no such thing as *closure*."

The definition for closure is "an act or process of closing something." Those who work with death, dying, grief, and trauma, understand that grieving is not a voluntary door that can be closed. Like a broken bone in our bodies, healing will occur, but there will be triggering periods. Despite the healing, there will be intermittent pain, spontaneous or even sharp memory, smells, sounds, or even seeing something that reminds us of the incident. It's baffling that the term 'closure' can be even remotely applied to grief, loss, bereavement, mourning and trauma.

Yet, popular culture has made it alive, and hopefully, that same culture will be part of its demise. The human part of ourselves, our hearts, remember those we have loved and lost. Our psyche remembers, and as long as we're on this mortal plane, nothing can change that fact. Although many have tried to put a therapeutic spin on 'closure,' I concur with rational-minded authors who emphatically assert that it does not exist in the clinical field of psychotherapy.

Mothers, victims, and survivors of gun violence trauma emphatically dismiss the false notion of the term with the varied explanations that come with it. We'll acknowledge closure as a cultural fad, a word created to minimize the intensity of grief and trauma. Traumatic grief is messy, painful, downright uncomfortable, and does not go away. The intensity of the emotions will subside; the pain will lessen over time; the impact of traumatic loss will diminish; we will notice an identifiable change, but the grief will never completely disappear.

I have observed firsthand how gradual acceptance, meaning-making, and legacy building have merged into empowerment.

The relationship that anyone has with a lost loved one remains as a relationship. Mothers continue to be mothers even if they only had one child who died. Although severed through death, that loving bond remains an essential part of their storying, as they reminisce, hold anniversaries, and share their grief journey. That bond will forever be a part of their existence until each one crosses the shores of death.

The dubiousness of *'closure'* in relation to grief, loss, and trauma, essentially negates it. Our culture seeks to dismiss one of the most integral connections we can ever have with loved ones who are a part of our existence. Where loving, human bonding has occurred, the mythic closure cannot sever those ties. No one has the right to impose words or project their discomfort on grievers who have the right to grieve, heal, and find meaningful acceptance at their own pace and in their own time, since we all grieve and heal differently.

Grief Languages

> *"Although it's always an unwanted guest, "Grief" does its painful, quiet, yet renewing job of change in every area of our lives with "Personal Gems" of lived experience. These 'little nuggets' become priceless to our growth and understanding."*
> **- Sky Starr (2010)**

Grief is generally termed an unwelcomed guest with its own universal language and an undesirable learning process. Smiles, tears, laughter, love, physical actions, and expressive reactions are *all* universal languages that "grief" utilizes.

Although grief cannot be spoken of as an employer, grief's modes of expressions employ verbal responses (written and oral);

nonverbal responses (silent or reflective); physical responses (somatic or expressions); and physical activities through rituals, ceremonies, or inordinate objects (Corless et al., 2014). Imageries, metaphors, and allegories constitute Grief's numerous colourful languages with diverse colours, figures, and analysis to capture its powerful impact.

Grief is also used and personified in the first person singular, and portrayed as a person who can act, think, speak, and move. Although everyone is acquainted with "it" as a process, when 'Grief' is mentioned, there's hallowed respect associated with it that cannot be missed or mistaken. Grief is also shown with a personal aspect, which speaks through various languages as 'it' manifests fluidly through human lives and consciousness.

Personifying "Grief" signifies a distinctive acknowledgement of Grief's ability to communicate universally without pomp or ceremony. But when one ponders human reactions, one must admit that Grief is not as silent as we would want or prefer it to be. Still, it begs to be expressed, using humanity and our modes of communication to utter universal languages. Shakespeare was no doubt inspired by Grief in coaxing people to *"give sorrow words."*

Starting with 'somatic expressions' through physical responses, Grief's language tells the story of the broken-hearted, traumatized, isolated, depressed, and lonely. The language of Grief can be heard from those whose pain still manifests in their silent withdrawal from socialization, through bouts of angry outlets, and the deep weltering sounds of distressed weeping.

Children are urged to use their intuitive imagination during expressive art to *'give sorrow words.'* During this process, a child's primitive expressions convey the internal wounds their vocabulary is yet to develop. This introductory approach to expressing and understanding an early death experience is vital for a child's mind, which aids in grasping the significance of their first encounter with death. Other modes of grief language expressions are thumb-sucking, bed-wetting, or insomnia. Where the child showed none of these expressive symptoms before, to the keen eye, grief's language is quite evident.

Allowing children to participate in ceremonies related to death also increases their vocabulary in other languages of grief. As that child grows older, those images from expressive art and acquired words or phrases are embedded in memory, hopefully with other positive pleasantries, observed from participation in ceremonies associated with loss. These formative but critical expressions, provide a paradigm for understanding the Modes of Expression of grief, making that child's grief expressions distinctive (Corless et al., 2014).

Where Grief Language is incorporated into youth behaviour patterns, a range of collective complaints speak for the sullen youth who intentionally shuts down; or the previously healthy youth who suddenly has a plethora of complaints from headaches, nausea, shortness of breath, dizziness, tightness in the chest to lethargy; those full-blown angry youth occasionally narrate their grief language with anticipated fears during moments of despair.

Youths' artistic portrayal of Grief Language can be seen through rap, music, art, and animated wardrobe, blending with pop culture as their symbol of honouring friends and family members. In recent times, youth also amplify social media, the internet, and other technological devices to speak Grief's Language. Facebook, Instagram, and Twitter are littered with Grief's Language as hearts brave an open platform, albeit 'behind the scenes,' to announce their loss, express their pain, and courageously speak their specific Grief Language.

Researchers agree that adulthood is the most common time for grief, mourning, and loss. Not only related to the ageing process, but many adults also take more significant risks, become complacent, and succumb to various diseases.

With years of acquired knowledge and exposure to death, grief, and loss, adults demonstrate a combination of Grief Languages with relatable symbolism, allegories, and modern artistry. Some adults openly discuss what they would like to see at their funeral, what type of funeral they would like to have, and purchase complete funeral/burial packages in advance.

I discuss my funeral with every appropriate opportunity. Although some of my family members would rather not discuss the topic, I continue to express what I would like to see done, what hymns I would like sung and have already picked out my outfit for my last rites.

Modern grief research branches out from these generalizations and recognizes the emotions associated with death and mourning as more complex. Unique approaches vary from person to person. Contemporary thoughts on grieving address individuality, pinpointing personal differences like gender, religious and cultural background, personality, social demographics, and environment. These elements play a different role in each person's unique expressions of grief and grieving processes.

John Adams caught a glimpse of how grief affects humanity with this poignant remark: *"Grief drives [people] into habits of serious reflection, sharpens the understanding, and softens the heart."*

CHAPTER 12

Prolonged Grief

Continued research on grief advances knowledge on the world's stage, as WHO released the inclusion of prolonged grief disorder (PGD) in its new International Classification of Diseases (ICD-11).

Prolonged grief disorder (PGD) is characterized by severe, persistent, and disabling grief. It is an unusually severe condition that impairs a person's ability to function in critical areas of life and functioning (Papazoglou, Konstantinos et al., 2020). Various cases relate to a child's sudden, violent death, among other instances (Nakajima et al., 2012; Burke and Meimeyer, 2014; Shear, 2015).

Prolonged grief leads to a multitude of emotional irregularities, which disrupt relationships and decrease levels of wellbeing. Even after 10 years, many gun violence survivors, and other violent homicides, have grave difficulty returning to work and social activities, at which they were previously adept or enjoyed. They are easily affected by death-related words, which trigger spontaneous ruminations, negative mood swings, and distressing memories.

Although PTSD and PGD have distinct symptoms, they overlap in certain instances, merging the dominant symptoms of fear, terror, and anxiety. PTSD symptoms combine sadness and yearning, the most prominent symptoms of prolonged grief. These symptoms relate to mothers whose sons' case is still in limbo, waiting for the *"elusive justice"* in their children's murders.

Mothers are especially disheartened by the continuous effects of prolonged grief. They frequently complain about the officer in charge of their case not returning any of the numerous calls they make. Regular grief consumes the griever to the point where that griever is submerged in thoughts, emotions and actions related to grief.

Traumatic, unexpected grief is magnified in severity and duration, often prolonged and, for most grievers, unbearable. A mother tormented with the "why's" of her son's loss is consumed with finding answers, and of course, achieving justice. Fairness, where understood before, is no longer affordable, nor is it a word that readily comes to mind. That mother is only concerned about what she's experiencing and the need she has.

Instead of trying to reason with distraught, impatient mothers by highlighting the obvious, such as:

1. The detective has other cases besides yours
2. There are other demands on an officer's day
3. He/She might be attending to a more recent case
4. The detective prefers to call when they have something new to report

We decided to have a teachable moment and invite a friendly neighbourhood officer to speak to our group.

The relationship between the police and marginalized communities is usually tense. Yet many understand that embodying safety must include an amicable relationship between law enforcement and the community. To improve conditions, we are cordially respectful to and consider 31 Division in our community as partners. We collaborate with them and cordially invite them to our events.

At one of our Interfaith Community Remembrance, an officer who had recently lost a parent joined mothers and the community in "diving grief." Dividing grief is a concept from Cicero's quote: *"Friendship improves happiness and abates misery, by the doubling of our joy and the dividing of our grief."* – Cicero. Grievers feel consoled and supported by others who share their presence.

Mothers expressed the camaraderie and kinship they felt with that officer who "seemed like a normal person in her own grief." Many of us tend to forget that people in positions, even those who might appear formidable, are human beings, possessing all the human frailties and emotions that regular folks have.

Having those officers attend and participate in our group was heart-warming, and I like to think that we made incremental steps to diffusing a bit of the customary tension. Our group sessions were quite interactive, and members were cordial and accommodating to the questions on police follow-up with cold case files. Like everyone else, officers are human beings with varied personalities.

One mother reported that she enjoyed periodic phone check-ins from the detective on her case, while another stated that she could expect a monthly update from the detective who had hers. Overall, mothers gained a better understanding of the processes surrounding cases and the demands on policemen's time.

Those who have lost a loved one to gun violence—mothers making up the majority—enter a more prolonged recovery trajectory, where elevated trauma responses make their journey feel like the new onset of grief. These symptoms are identified by traits synonymous with their initial reactions to the death.

Their emotions remain intense with anger, grieving, and continuous weepiness; preoccupation with the death, yearning, longing, and flashbacks of memories experienced daily; inability to function on the social, occupational, and other important aspects of ADL (activities of daily living).

Culturally, the duration of symptoms exceeds the customarily expected time frame (Shear, 2012). One key indicator is the refusal and incapability of re-engaging in ADL. Mothers suffering from prolonged grief usually compare their loss with another person's, without realizing they need to allow "Grief's Work" to be done.

Cold cases

The Toronto Police Services (TPS) website includes a long list of cold cases, including a *'rewards section'* requesting public support and or tips leading to arrests for cases dating back to 1980.

> "Statistically, homicide investigators have been very successful in solving murders in Toronto. Overall, clearance rates, although varying year over year, have averaged near 80 percent from 1921 until now."

This report from TPS holds little significance for the many mothers who are stuck with prolonged grief. They remain preoccupied with their loss, and struggle with the daily stressors of knowing that someone is freely enjoying their life while their child is dead. Toronto Crime Stoppers is a not-for-profit organization seeking to build "a partnership between public, police and the media." Their chair, Sean Sportun, upholds that "Homicides and crimes against children are usually awarded the most—reward—for successful tips."

Dating back to 2001, 20 mothers I know are still waiting, hoping, and praying for justice for their sons. Periodically, the police spotlights a "cold case," plead for witnesses, and offers "a reward for information leading to a particular case's arrest and conviction." Still, most gun-related deaths remain in the cold case files. At the same time, mothers are incapacitated, complaining of mental exhaustion, as they continuously yearn for justice that will usher desired healing.

However, where traumatic deaths occur, the emotions of relief, release, and restoration take on different meanings. Pent-up emotions are held in the state of homeostasis. In biological terms, homeostasis is "the state of steady internal, physical, and chemical conditions maintained by living systems."

Restoration for family and mothers, incorporates a revised version of re-engagement after a traumatic loss, which happens in stages. The scarcity of resources and community based grief support to meet survivors' complex and long-term trauma needs leave mothers, families, and communities with unaddressed, debilitating psycho-social challenges and prolonged grief. The expectation of *"justice"* bears heavily on a survivor's healing process.

Most violent gun deaths happen to youth who had no issues with the law; youth who, according to society's standards, have "kept their nose clean;" innocent children and others killed by stray bullets. These family members crave the "mysterious justice," which assists in their healing. Where justice is not meted out or forthcoming, folks develop bitterness, indifference to the process, and plummet into prolonged grief.

Rare Justice

Receiving "satisfaction" from a child's murder is a "RARE" commodity. Many mothers spend sleepless nights waiting, wondering, and hoping against hope that the person responsible for their child's death will be caught and brought to justice. Some mothers never get to see their child's body after the death, which further complicates their trauma and keeps them in prolonged grief.

A young woman was killed by a boyfriend she only knew for two and a half months. Newspapers across the city relayed the gruesome tale in graphic detail, which both horrified and enthralled public interest.

While such news implanted piqued interest to others, it was sheer devastation to a mother, sibling, and other immediate families. A beloved daughter, sister, aunt, cousin, friend, and co-worker was suddenly and violently snatched from their lives. Emotions attached to such sudden, drastic finality have crippling effects on trauma survivors.

The layered levels of dread, anxieties, and fears that survivors experience cannot be justified with words. Mothers relay how they never thought they'd be burying their children. It's abnormal to the natural course of life.

With humbled privilege, I journeyed with this mother through pain, trauma, retraumatization and six long, tedious weeks of a murder trial.

We had preparation sessions where I tried to anticipate emotions that might arise and how the courtroom setting might be intimidating. The prosecutor reminded her of how significant her presence in the courtroom was and will be to the case, and even advised her to refrain from an outburst when the verdict is finally read at the end of the trial; we explored emotions that would unnerve and even rattle her balance, but no amount of preparation is ever sufficient.

This mother had accepted the challenge. She not only wanted to have answers to the parade of tormented questions about her daughter's death, but she also sought justice for her daughter. Her presence in court meant that she was speaking for, and demanding justice for a daughter who could neither speak nor demand it for herself.

She strategically sat at the back of the courtroom to make hasty retreats when necessary. The weighty silences between testimonies, cross-examinations, and questions from the judge were deafening. This mother, however, carried the weightiest amount of tangled, raw emotions known to humanity. Yet, she was fueled by the pursuit of justice.

There were times when this mother's ears and heart couldn't accept or listen to the horrid details and boastful reports of how her daughter was killed. Occasionally, she hastily left the room as the dam of her traumatized heart overflowed.

Although bitter-sweet, the desired justice was decisive. The determined sentence of 25 years to life was a rare smile from the justice system, but at what cost? A mother now faced the laboriously difficult and dreary strides to attain emotional healing. A sense of satisfaction, yes! Justice? Finally! Justice in its rare form for one mother! The painful realization is that neither justice nor satisfaction can ever replace her daughter. Now the long journey of restoration and healing begins.

Recommendations and Conclusion

> *"Violence is not an inherent part of the human condition. It can be predicted and prevented. In recent decades, data-driven and evidence-based approaches have produced knowledge and strategies that can prevent violence. These include interventions at [governmental],*

individual, close relationship, community and societal levels" WHO (2017).

Compared to 2005, when Paul Martin promised a national ban during his election campaign, the count was at 350,000 for legally owned handguns across the country. Today there are more than 1 million, not including the illegal guns flooding the border and infiltrating communities (Toronto Star, 2020).

It has been well-documented that Canada lags significantly behind countries like England, New Zealand, Australia, and Switzerland, which swiftly set laws and restrictions to protect their citizens. The slow, tedious process of setting positive, reactionary measures to assist community patrons continues to cost lives. This trajectory needs to be replaced with swifter actions that place value on lives lost and the families and communities that are continuously affected.

In 2019, Toronto's Medical Officer of Health made the following impressive recommendations, entitled "Community Violence in Toronto: A Public Health Approach" (HL11-1, 2019). They highlight the extreme need for immediate implementation as forecasted.

Implications for the community will be integrated between these recommendations to identify gaps while lending input where applicable.

1. *Identify, collect, and review data on the impacts of community violence for appropriate action by Toronto Public Health and other City Divisions.*

My recommendation:

Policymakers frequently decide what the community needs, often without listening to, or hearing directly from the community itself. Organizations like Out Of Bounds have responded to gun-related crises since the 'Year of the Gun.' We have conducted research and collected data in collaboration with scholars from Ryerson University, Women's College Hospital, and other affiliates. The community must be consulted, informed, and allowed to provide input on any potential program and services for youth and the community.

2. *Bring a public health perspective and identify issues to inform the Community Safety and Wellbeing Plan.*

My recommendation:

Gun violence needs to be identified and declared as the epidemic it is. The steady increase in activities, the accumulated number of deaths, and the scope of incidents have been evident to families and communities since the late 1990s. Many decried Jane Creba's death, while there was and continues to be silence on lives lost in marginalized communities, without recognition.

Gun violence has surged in recent years with amplified ferocity. Toronto Public Health's (TPH) analysis shows an alarming increase in firearm activities from 2013 to 2017. The crime rate more than doubled for youth and adults. Emergency departments recorded over 102,000 emergency visits with 1,133 visits for a firearm-related injury. We are ineffectual without recognizing and admitting to the devastating lethal epidemic of gun violence, while the community deals with the brunt of repetitive gun deaths.

3. *Develop and engage a child and youth component in that safety plan; engage children and youth in the development process.*

My recommendation:

The basic human need of "safety and security" has been as elusive as justice. Children and youth in marginalized communities live with a daily, constant fear for their lives. They also have a keen sense of what's happening around them and articulate their specific needs concerning safety and security. Their voices must undoubtedly be included in activities involving their wellbeing. Not in written documents or glib mentions, but consulting with and documenting their perspectives.

Adults, officials, and those who sincerely want to be proactive must adopt a youth-centric approach in planning, implementation, evaluation, building partnerships, communication, and governance.

4. *Adopt Bill 129 to amend the Health Insurance Act and the Health Protection and Promotion Act to address gun violence and its impacts to increase hospital-based violence interventions and affordable trauma-informed mental health supports to individuals exposed to violence.*

My recommendation:

This huge gap in services for gun-related injuries and deaths has been burdensome, and continues to be a significant health risk for ostracized communities. Injured parties are discharged from hospital, and left on their own to manage and heal.

The psychological trauma further compounds their healing, adding extra strains on families, caregivers, and injured parties. Youth are the primary subjects whose lives are irrevocably damaged after injury. The provincial disability insurance structure is nonexistent to cover costs for long-term care. Survivors rely on family, friends, and other means of support. Wrap-around care with trauma-informed therapy, home care for their injuries, and rehabilitation services must be constructed to assist recovery.

5. *Urging the federal government to ban the sale of handgun ammunition in Toronto, consistent with the City Council's decision in June 2019 on Item EX6.7, City Powers to Regulate Firearms and Ammunition.*

My recommendation:

"Under the Ontario Ammunition Regulation Act, 1994, and the Imitation Firearms Act, 2000, the province regulates or prohibits the sale of ammunition, deactivated firearms and imitation firearms to individuals under 18 years of age." (June 18, 19, 2019).

Put forward on May 29, 2019; this motion was adopted in June 2019. Toronto communities dealing with gun violence occurrences with eminent deaths, and the traumatic after-effects of trauma, don't have the luxury of prolonged wait periods before a bylaw is enacted. Toronto can look to New Zealand as an exemplary model of swift action regarding gun control and protect its citizens by banning handguns.

6. *Urging the federal government to prohibit the availability, sale, possession and use of handguns, assault rifles and semi-automatic firearms in Canada, consistent with the City Council's decision in June 2019 on Item EX6.7.*

My recommendation:

Most shooting occurrences and deaths in communities are from handguns. Listed under "Related Advice," number 25, in the Alvin Curling's Report of 2008, a ban on handguns was among the recommendations, which 13 years later, is yet to be enacted.

> To reduce the risk of serious violence where those interventions have not been made or have not succeeded, the Province should continue to press the federal

government to implement a handgun ban in Ontario, and should also explore every feasible initiative it might take itself to minimize the risks while the federal government continues to permit these guns in Ontario apartments and homes. (Executive Summary, 2008)

Although firearms are federally regulated in Canada, handguns are responsible for all gun-related homicides in communities. In 1995, *Bill C-68* was ratified after a gunman murdered 14 female engineering students at the École Polytechnique de Montréal on December 6, 1989.

On July 16, 2012, the Danzig Street shooting in Scarborough saw two fatalities and 24 injuries when a 9mm pistol, .40 calibre and an Uzi submachine gun were deliberately fired on a crowd of 200 at a block party. On July 22, 2018, the gunman killed two people and wounded 13, using a Smith & Weston M&P .40-calibre handgun.

Unlike the situation where *Bill C-68* was ratified, no laws were introduced to address the carnage in Toronto. Despite the recent ban on assault rifles, Toronto, Ontario, and Canada are overdue for an overhaul of the handguns killing youth and snuffing innocent lives in underserved and undervalued communities and nationally.

7. *Request the federal government to identify and assess criteria for addressing social determinants of health when it comes to its project through the National Crime Prevention granting program/ strategy;*

My recommendation:

Canada prides itself on being one of the healthiest countries in the world, yet some Canadians are healthier and have more opportunities to lead a healthy life (Oct. 7, 2020). People from the

Black, Indigenous, and other People of Colour (BIPOC)—deal with an ongoing undercurrent of the root causes of community violence, which in some cases are blatant.

Poverty, racism, racial/ethnic and gender inequities; discrimination, stigmatization, oppression; lack of economic opportunities, increased unemployment, over-representation in police scrutiny, and self-stigmatization are among the lengthy list of the social determinants of health affecting the BIPOC community.

The province and Toronto, must address the level of poverty in *[disadvantaged communities],* their concentrations, and the many discriminatory circumstances that accompany it. In addition to reducing poverty, promote economic integration by ensuring affordable, good quality housing. Substantially improve the most disadvantaged communities as well, enabling people to maintain residency rather than seeking economic pursuits in different neighbourhoods.

8. *Request Statistics Canada to collect representative data on the exposure to community violence at the municipal level identify and assess criteria for addressing the social determinants of health through national surveys, Canadian Community Health, and Children and Youth surveys to analyze the health and other impacts of community violence.*

My recommendation:

Gun violence appears to be most noticed when multiple people die at once. Yet, gun violence and its detrimental effects distress many people within communities, where many live in constant fear of the next incident or impending death.

Black residents have an unemployment rate of 12 percent, which alarmingly is nearly double the provincial rate; there's an overrepresentation of Black residents on social services.

Truancy, school suspensions, and academic streaming with early dropouts are significantly high. It has been established that Black, Indigenous, People of Colour (BIPOC) are seen as "the minority" and treated as such.

The City of Toronto needs to pressure both the provincial and the federal governments to respond to shootings in Toronto with the same enactment to ban handguns, which are prevalent in most shooting deaths and gang-related activities.

Community-based, collaborative, problem-solving models to address gun violence trauma must seek to blend prevention strategies with practicality. Customized service delivery that substantiates the need for post-traumatic care in the educational, systemic and policymaking arenas must also be tabled, recognized, and validated in these interventions. Such fundamental changes will do justice to survivors and encourage a constructive approach in meeting the complex traumatic needs of mothers and their families.

Unrelenting gun-violent deaths indicate the need for cathartic intervention, which is portrayed in the unspoken actions of anguished youths, anxious parents, and frontline workers, overwhelmed by the enormity of complicated grief within their communities. Such intervention will provide grief support, education, an environment of safety and security that will foster healing within a context where the anxiety levels are maximized.

A proactive approach for gun violence from Toronto, will see therapeutic, acquired empirical data tailored, with improved implementation of advanced knowledge, to minimize and alleviate the psychological vulnerabilities that are very evident among youth and families in marginalized communities.

Given the high levels of mental distress that follow grotesque losses from gun violence, it is imperative that all levels of government seriously collaborate to diminish and appease these stressors. Survivors, caregivers, frontline workers, and clinicians must be consulted to assess and intervene, with the intent to empower and instill a keen sense of hope for youth, families, and communities experiencing encrusted, complicated grief.

Without adequate support, hope and healing through therapeutic and societal efforts, there is little chance that people can mobilize to "meaning-making" or create a better future for themselves or their communities.

Conclusion

> "We are now forced with the fact that tomorrow is today. **We are confronted with the fierce urgency of now.** In this unfolding conundrum of life and history, there "is" such a thing as being too late. This is no time for apathy or complacency. This is a time for vigorous and positive action."
> - Dr. Martin Luther King, Jr. (1963).

Since the Year of the Gun in 2005, Toronto has been in *"the fierce urgency of now."* People in places of authority—those in positions to bring about tangible change—glibly use phrases such as "this issue is a priority to this government…" without further actions to authenticate that stance.

There is an urgency for politicians, policymakers, leaders, community workers, and advocates to engage in perceptible acts to preserve young lives, and work at preventing unceasing traumatic pain to youth, mothers, families, and communities.

The ferocious struggle against gun violence trauma continues to deteriorate families and communities. Research repeatedly acknowledges that living in violent communities compromises residents' ability to break intergenerational cycles of violence. Without large-scale interventions, a neighbourhood becomes effectively unable to protect itself against the perpetuation of a culture that is normed in violence. (Violence Policy, 2017). It is widely observed and recognized that there is no **'after-care'** for the post-traumatic stress experienced by many after a gun incident.

Gun violence, with the trauma that ensues and the post-care needed, are inexhaustible topics which leave individuals and the entire communities unprepared for the loss and trauma that follows. Canada's official emergency preparedness guide urges families to "*be prepared to take care of yourself and your family for a minimum of 72 hours*" if an emergency happens in their community because "*it may take emergency workers some time to reach you.*" *(*Date modified: 2021-05-07).

Although the above notice refers to a disaster or catastrophe, communities with repetitive gun violence and deaths are in a continuous *'state of emergency,'* with no relief in sight. Trauma has no boundaries concerning age, gender, socioeconomic status, race, ethnicity, or sexual orientation. Recent shootings in the community left four people injured, including three children, at a toddler's birthday party. (Freeman, CP24, June 21, 2021). For the past two concessive Sundays, someone has been shot and killed in the same area, within the community.

Albert Camus aptly stated that "*This time is a time in which children, youth and communities suffer, but we can lessen the number of suffering children; we can lessen the number of suffering youth; we can lessen the number of suffering families, and we must seek to lessen the number of suffering communities.*" (Adapted, Rev. Sky; Oct. 28, 2013)

Closing Commentary

ARDENE, ROBINSON VOLLMAN

Dr. Ardene Robinson Vollman, PhD, is adjunct associate professor (retired) at the University of Calgary. Ardene has served in various public health arenas and is past Chair of the Canadian Public Health Association Board. She is the editor of *Canadian Community as Partner: Theory and Multidisciplinary Practice*, now in its 5th Edition.

As Canadians, we take pride that we live in a nonviolent and safe country even though we share the world's longest undefended border with the world's largest manufacturer of guns. The US commands a staggering rate of gun violence—which claims over 30,000 lives annually—and the American Public Health Association (APHA) has declared gun violence an urgent public health issue that demands an effective evidence-based policy response (2018).

Recently, Canada has experienced a rise in illegal guns and shootings, resulting in deaths and injuries and a decreased sense of safety. According to the National Police Federation (NPF), in 2019, 2,242 illegally sold guns used in crimes in Canada were traced back to manufacturers in the United States (NPF, 2020 citing USDOJ, 2020). According to Statistics Canada (2019a, 2020), there were 678 homicides in 2019, of which 38% were gun-related fatal shootings.

Gun-related homicides have risen over the past decade, fueled in part by gang violence and organized crime, and are particularly prominent in inner cities (StatsCan, 2019b). Handguns, primarily prohibited or restricted in Canada, have been the most common firearm used in gun-related deaths. Canada's experience with gun violence is significantly different from our southern neighbour, explained in part by the differential access to firearms in the two countries.

On January 30, 2021, The Toronto Star published "Under the Gun" about Toronto's neighbourhood gun violence (Ngabo & Plana, 2021). In the article, Reverend Sky Starr was featured, revealing her response to gunshots heard in her neighbourhood and her professional concern about the trauma that gun violence has on the community.

Rev. Sky Starr founded "Out Of Bounds," a charitable organization that provides free programs to support mothers and survivors of gun violence in the Jane-Finch area and the GTA. She collaborates with other community groups and others dedicated to eliminating gun violence through community interventions and support.

The Canadian Public Health Association (CPHA) has no official policy statement about gun violence. However, at a public forum at Public Health 2017 in Halifax, Ian Culbert, Executive Director of CPHA, said: "We know that violence is often a symptom of larger problems, and so we look at those upstream issues, such as education, income, housing, that can lead to violence, and so that's a public health approach to violence prevention." He called for investment in community centres, education, and quality housing.

Swannie Jett (2016), of the National Association of County and City Health Officials (NACCHO), states: [Gun violence] can be prevented through a comprehensive public health approach that keeps families and communities safe.

NACCHO supports core public health activities necessary to eradicate gun violence:

(1) conducting surveillance to track firearm-related deaths, determine causes, and assess intervention methods;
(2) identifying risk factors associated with gun violence (e.g., poverty and depression) and resilience or protective factors that guard against violence (e.g., youth access to trusted adults);
(3) developing, implementing, and evaluating interventions to decrease risk factors and build resilience; and
(4) institutionalizing successful prevention strategies.

A public health approach to gun violence prevention and trauma-focused therapy is needed to address the effects of gun violence on those affected by the loss and injury that result in family and community suffering. In this publication, Rev. Sky Starr shares her experience of supporting those healing efforts.

We can all learn from her insights.

Glossary of Terminology

A

Abbreviated Grief:

A very brief period of grief where a griever mourns for the lost loved one but appears to have gone through the grieving process and claims to have no residual pain related to the loss. This type of grief is rare and can be attributed to two factors:

a) The griever has replaced the lost person with someone else or

b) The attachment to the lost person was emotionally short-lived

Although the griever appears to have "moved on in life," there are intermittent periods where the pangs of loss would still affect that person.

Absent Grief
Grief where someone shows minimal response to a loss and seems to be in no emotional distress. Usually appears as a dismissed reaction or as denial or avoidance of the loss.

Active Coping
"Active" coping describes the *active* actions done to reduce the stressors' negative impact on mental health. *Active coping* could be changing surroundings or adapting one's inner or behavioural responses to the loss.

Accountability Partner
A person who listens to, accompanies, and encourages another person during a crisis or emotionally difficult time, especially during "triggers," helping them maintain equilibrium.

Advocacy
Speaking on someone's behalf or performing a social act that protects and advances the rights of others on a human, legal, or social level.

Agony
The intense mental and emotional suffering that someone experiences; usually used to describe grievers feelings, and the intense emotions at the onset of fresh grief.

Ambiguous Loss
Coined by Dr. Pauline Boss in the 1970s. A loss that occurs without resolution or clear understanding, leaving people searching for explanations. It complicates and delays the grieving process and often results in unresolved grief.

Anam Cara
Anam Cara means **"Soul Friend."** Anam is the *Gaelic* word for soul, and Cara is the word for friend. (Wikipedia, 2020).

Anguish
Extreme unhappiness caused by physical or mental suffering. Anguish is felt physically and emotionally during a tragedy.

Anxiety
Feelings of fear and apprehension accompanied by physical and emotional side effects.

Anticipatory Grief
The grief experienced when a family member is diagnosed with a terminal illness with no cure.

Anticipatory Trauma Reaction
A future-focused form of distress from dwelling on media reports and discussions of impending gun violence. Youth and families living in marginalized communities experience this constant state of anticipatory trauma reactions daily.

B

Bereavement
The condition experienced when someone loses a loved one to death. It introduces grief and the grieving process. This state causes emotional pain, mental anguish, and distress, including weepiness.

Bereavement Hallucination
During acute grief, close family members reveal seeing, hearing, and sensing the presence of a dead loved one.

Bereavement Overload
The term "bereavement overload" was coined by psychologist and gerontologist Robert Kastenbaum in the late 1900s. It refers to a situation where a griever must deal with multiple losses in rapid succession, without processing each loss.

Black Death/Plague
Also known as the Pestilence, Great Bubonic Plague, the Great Plague, the Plague, or less commonly the Black Plague. One of the most devastating pandemics in human history, resulting in the deaths of an estimated 75 to 200 million people in Eurasia, peaking in Europe from 1347 to 1351. The bacterium Yersinia pestis, which results in several forms of plague, is believed to have been the cause (Crawford, 2018).

Buddy System
A model of care created and customized by Rev. Sky Starr and the 'Out Of Bounds' group—*G-Social*—to assist mothers on their healing journey.

C

Chronic Grief
The grief period is longer than what is considered normal. It happens when acceptance of the loss doesn't occur, making it impossible for the griever to proceed through the stages of grief.

Closure
A misconception often used concerning grief. There is no closure in grief. **Definition:** "An act or process of closing something, especially an institution, thoroughfare, or frontier, or of being closed." (Webster's Dictionary). Closure does not relate to grief.

Collective Grief
Grief experienced by communities, villages, nations, and societies after an individual, multiple loss, or disaster that causes mass casualties and creates widespread tragedy. Collective grief evokes helplessness and hopelessness due to the lack of control over these heartbreaks and the powerlessness to prevent them.

Community
Generally viewed as a group of people living in geographic proximity sharing common needs and interests (Stamler & Yiu, 2008).

Complicated Grief
An inability to function normally because of grief. Studies find that complicated grief endures several years for some bereaved people.

Compounded Grief
Experienced when all the losses over a period of time are combined. People experiencing this type of grief sink quickly into depression over another tragic event or death.

Confusion
People are uncertain about what to do, or cannot comprehend something clearly: they don't understand what's happening, what's expected, or what's to be done.

Crisis
A sudden, unexpected tragedy which leads to an unstable and dangerous situation affecting individuals, groups, communities, or society.

Cross-Cultural Differences
Variations in meaning or expression of thoughts, feelings, or behaviours related to ethnic or religious identity or place of origin.

Cry
To make sad noises along with *tears*, to yell loudly, or moan while shedding tears.

Cultural Competence
Coined by Laura S. Brown in 2008, cultural competence is the therapist's capacity to be self-aware regarding their own identities and cultural norms. The therapist's ability to be sensitive to the nuances of the realities of human difference and possess an epistemology of difference allows for creative responses to the client.

Cultural Sensitivity
Knowledge, awareness, and acceptance of other cultures and cultural identities.

Cumulative Grief
The occurrence of multiple deaths, either simultaneously or in succession, giving no time for a griever to process emotions. It causes an overwhelming emotional response from a griever or caretaker.

D

Death
The end of life. Death is the permanent, irreversible cessation of all biological functions that sustain a human being or living organism. It is an inevitable, universal process that occurs in all living beings or things.

Death Anxiety
Refers to the fear and anxiety related to the anticipation and awareness of dying, death, or becoming nonexistent.

Debriefing
Relates to a routine, individual or group review of an event, which provides an objective perspective for assessing strengths, weaknesses and areas that need improvement. Often used in early crisis response, follow up and management.

Delayed Grief
Like 'postponed grief,' this type of grief is simply on hold while the griever focuses on other things they have deemed more important. Since everyone grieves in their unique way, this is seen as a normal process.

Desensitization
A diminishing of emotional responsiveness to negative or positive stimuli after being exposed to them for a while.

Despair
The feeling of complete loss or absence of hope; a sense of hopelessness.

Disenfranchised Grief
Also known as hidden grief, dismissed suffering, or sorrow that is unacknowledged or invalidated by social norms.

Dissociation
A break in how one's mind handles information. One may feel disconnected from thoughts, feelings, memories, and surroundings. This disconnection is automatic and entirely out of one's control.

Distorted Grief
When the intense pain of loss seems too much to handle, some turn these emotions inwardly to themselves, exhibiting self-hate and self-anger. As a form of complicated grief, these emotions show a drastic behaviour change. Guilt, anger, and hostility are among the most prominent behaviours.

Dividing Grief
Having friends and family around not only consoles but comforts a griever. Emotions are less intense when friends are there to support, which can be termed "dividing grief," making it less painful.

DSM-5
The Diagnostic and Statistical Manual of Mental Disorders, 5th Edition (DSM-5) is the product of more than 10 years of effort by hundreds of international experts in all aspects of mental health. Their dedication and hard work have yielded an authoritative volume that defines and classifies mental disorders to improve diagnoses, treatment, and research (DSM-5, 2020).

E

Ebb and Flow
A wave of recurring or rhythmical patterns that come and go. Grief's *'ebb'* refers to the receding or lessening of intense emotions. Grief's *'flow'* relates to the sudden upsurge, or grief trigger when memories erupt, and the griever experiences a **S.T.U.G.** (**S**udden **T**raumatic **U**psurge of **G**rief) reaction.

Epistemology
The branch of philosophy concerned with knowledge. It's the theory of knowledge, especially relating to its methods, validity, and scope.

Exaggerated Grief
A rare type of complicated grief referring to a cluster of symptoms that continues in high intensity for at least six months after a loss, creating extreme difficulty with daily activities and function. It's also classified as *"persistent complex bereavement disorder,"* in the *Diagnostic and Statistical Manual (DSM-5)*. Exaggerated grief emerges from excessive pain and an inability to cope.

F

Facilitator
Someone who helps bring about an outcome (such as learning, productivity, or communication) by providing indirect or discreet assistance, guidance, or supervision.

Family Therapy
A type of psychotherapy that helps family members better understand each other, support one another, and work through difficult situations. It involves all members of a nuclear family or stepfamily and, in some cases, extended family members (e.g., grandparents). Sessions are conducted one-on-one, in couples, or groups. The web of interpersonal relationships is examined, and communication is strengthened within the family.

Fresh Grief
Sharp emotional pain after learning of a death. Absence and other stressors come with such a loss within the first year of that loss.

Freshman Griever
A person experiencing fresh grief and is also in the first year of their grief journey. Coined by Rev. Sky Starr, (Sept. 2007).

Frozen Grief
The grief felt from an unresolved or uncertain loss. Grief when a very close friend or a loved one is missing—presumed dead—whose whereabouts are unknown and unresolved, and there is significant potential for a bad outcome.

G

Gender
The differentiating and range of characteristics between (female) femininity and (male) masculinity. The term relates to the socially constructed concepts (male and female) based on appearances, thoughts, actions, and behaviours, especially when considering social and cultural differences rather than biological ones (Webster's).

Gender-Responsive
Refers to outcomes that reflect an understanding of gender roles and inequalities and encourages equal participation and fair distribution of benefits. Gender responsiveness is accomplished through gender analysis and gender inclusiveness.

Grief
Intense sorrow or sadness caused by losing a loved one—especially by death or the loss of possession with sentimental value.

Grief-Dividers
Friends who accompany grievers during the rough patches of the grief journey through supportive listening and encouragement.

Grief Overload
Experiencing too many significant losses within proximity to each other, without enough time to process the grief or heal. Unlike 'normal' grief, multiple losses create substantial stress and anxiety

with emotional pain, which needs time to be psychologically processed.

Grief-Related
Profound and poignant distress caused by, or associated with grief, loss, or bereavement.

Grief-Related Memory Loss
Memory loss associated with grief or because of grieving. It usually happens within the first year of grief but differs for each griever. Seen as a temporary situation, but the length of time varies with the uniqueness of grief.

Grief Response
The overwhelming emotional pain that's felt when someone has died. Depending on the closeness of the relationship to the person who died, emotional reactions may include shock, anger, disbelief, guilt, blame, and profound sadness.

Grief Guilt
Emotions of remorse and self-blame, expressed by survivors who often feel that if they had been there or done something differently, they might have been able to prevent the death of their loved one (OOB G-Social Group).

Gun Violence
The broadly defined category of violence and crime committed with a firearm (Webster, 1998).

I

Inhibited Grief
The suppression of the natural responses to the emotional pain of losing someone; restrained grief that's held back or prevented

from being revealed. Human beings need outlets for every type of painful emotion. When grief is 'inhibited' (prevented), the griever makes a conscious effort to either disregard the loss, or refuse to allow their feelings to be displayed. Shock can also inhibit emotions from being expressed. Where such a situation is prolonged, physical symptoms that generally accompany grief intensify.

Intergenerational Trauma
Trauma that is passed down from those who directly experienced an incident to subsequent generations, who learn about the trauma. Sometimes referred to as *'trans-or multigenerational trauma.'*

L

Longing The powerful feeling, need and desire to see, hear, or touch a lost one who has died; having an intense yearning for something or someone another person from whom they've been separated.
Loss This term is not limited to death and is defined as "the harm, trouble, and sadness etc. caused by losing someone or something (particularly through death)."

M

Marginalize Relegated to a marginal position within a society or group. Before 1970, *"marginalize"* took on the meaning that is most widely known today, "to relegate to an unimportant or powerless position" (that is, to the metaphorical margins of society).

Use of the word can be found as far back as 1968. An article in *The Los Angeles Times* from June 20th of that year reports, "[T]he Negro was kept aside, *marginalized*, thus composing in its large majority the chronically poor." In its newer sense, *marginalization* has assumed a much more prominent vocabulary than it once had. (Mariam Webster, 2020)

Masked Grief
Situations where the griever has become adept at suppressing their feelings of emotional pain, while taking on other symptoms. It is seen as a type of grief reaction when a person experiences symptoms and behaviours that cause them difficulty, but does not see or recognize that these are related to their loss.

Memory Loss (short-term)
A person can remember incidents from 20 years ago but is unsure of what happened 20 minutes ago.

Mental Health
A person's overall psychological and emotional wellbeing.

Mental Health First Aid
Training that teaches people how to offer initial supportat the onset of a crisis, until appropriate professional help is received or until the crisis is resolved.

Misery
Distress or suffering caused by need, deprivation, poverty, marginalization, or gun violence death.

Mourning
To feel, experience and express grief or sorrow; to show the typical signs of distress for death especially, with tears, weeping, moaning. It's identified with cultural norms such as wearing black clothes, armbands, ribbons etc.

O

Ostracism
Refers to the act of ignoring and excluding individuals. Differentiated from social exclusion, it demonstrates lack of attention in addition to '*social*' exclusion.

Outreach
A collection of mental health services extended to survivors wherever they gather to understand common coping reactions, and receive more in-depth help.

P

Parental Grief
The pain and deep sorrow felt by a mother or father whose child has died. The emotion includes the *bereavement* of *parents* who have experienced a stillbirth or fetus from a miscarriage.

Perceived Stigma
The fear of being discriminated against, or the fear of endorsed stigma arising from society's belief.

Persistent Complex Bereavement Disorder
Characterized by unshakeable grief that does not follow the general pattern of improvement over time. Individuals continue to experience persistent and intense emotions or moods, and unusually severe symptoms that impair functioning, or cause extreme psychological pain.

Prevention/Intervention
Prevention includes a wide range of activities—known as **"interventions"**—to reduce risks or threats to health. There are three categories of **prevention**: primary, secondary, and tertiary.

- **Primary Prevention:** trying to prevent gun violence, injury, and death.
- **Secondary Prevention:** efforts to detect violence early and prevent it from getting worse.
- **Tertiary Prevention:** actions to improve quality of life and reduce the symptoms and devastation of gun-related trauma (APA, 2005).

Primary/ Direct Victims
Generally refers to direct family and/or individuals immediately involved in a situation.

Post-Traumatic Growth (PTG)
A theory explaining a type of transformation following trauma. It was developed by psychologists Richard Tedeschi, PhD, and Lawrence Calhoun, PhD, in the mid-1990s, and holds that people who endure psychological struggle following adversity can often see growth afterward (APA, 2016).

Prolonged Grief
Prolonged Grief Disorder (PGD) is a characteristic of distressing, disabling yearning that persists a year or more after the loss. (Annual Reviews, 2021). PGD is a diagnostic entity now included in the *International Classification of Diseases 11th Revision* (ICD-11) and soon to appear in the *Diagnostic and Statistical Manual of Mental Disorders*, fifth edition, text revision (DSM-5-TR).

Psychological Debriefing
Used to describe a variety of structured events led by a person or team. It includes education, assessment, and review processes, with a strong focus on coping strategies and resilience.

Psychological First Aid (PFA)
Practical interventions with survivors and/or crisis responders to identify acute stress reactions at the onset of a crisis, and provide immediate supports where needed.

R

Racial
Groupings of human beings who are divided and recognized by physical appearance and other characteristics.

Rekindled Trauma
The resurgence of an old traumatic situation, or a trigger, causing that pain to resurface with the action of a new problem that resembles the initial trauma.

Re-storying
A therapeutic process where clients are encouraged to replace a negative image—imagined or real—with a pleasant memory of their loved one.

Retraumatization
A relapse into a state of trauma, triggered by a subsequent event that relates to, or reminds a person of the initial trauma they experienced.

Ripple Effects
A situation where one event produces effects, and other subsequent effects follow.

Risk Factors
Empirically validated variables related to risk for long-term adjustment problems such as severity and type of traumatic exposure, injuries, or sudden unexpected death of loved one(s).

Includes separation from family, previous psychological disorder, age, socioeconomic class, chronic mental illness, residential relocation, severe post-traumatic reactions, degree of resource losses, and community resource loss.

S

Sadness
An emotional pain associated with, or characterized by feelings of loss, despair, grief, helplessness, disappointment, and sorrow. Visible signs of **sadness** may include quietness, lethargy, and withdrawal.

Sanctuary Trauma
The emotional impulse that results when an individual directly or indirectly hears of, or observers the firsthand trauma experiences of another person. It occurs when an individual, who suffered a severe stressor, encounters what was expected to be a supportive and 'protective environment' only to discover more trauma. Developed by Dr. Steven Silver in 2005.

Secondary Trauma
Indirect exposure to trauma through a firsthand account or narrative of a traumatic event. Also referred to as compassion fatigue, (CF), or vicarious trauma (VT).

Secondary/Indirect Traumatization
A potential effect of "exposure" to individuals who have been adversely affected by traumatic stressors. It may occur when family members or groups of victims are in the process of helping trauma victims.

Secondary/Indirect Victims
Generally refers to individuals with close family and personal ties to primary victims.

Self-Stigma
The process in which a person becomes aware of public stigma, agrees with those stereotypes, and internalizes them by applying them to the self (Corrigan, Larson, & Kuwabara, 2010).

Shock
A sudden or violent mental and emotional disturbance that disrupts the equilibrium, causing emotional, intellectual, physical, and spiritual imbalance; being so disturbed that all motor functions stop.

Sibling Loss
The death of a biological brother, sister, or an adopted sibling. This loss is known to trigger intensely unresolved guilt, rivalry, and abandonment, especially if that sibling was a twin.

Social Determinants of Health (SDH)
The non-medical factors that influence health outcomes. Conditions in which people are born, grow, work, live, and age, and the broader set of forces and systems shaping the conditions of daily life (WHO, 2015).

Social Ostracization
Refers to the act of ignoring and excluding individuals. It is differentiated from social exclusion, in that it requires ignoring or lack of attention, in addition to social exclusion.

Social Stigma
The disapproval of, or discrimination against a person, based on perceivable social characteristics that distinguish them from other members of society.

Glossary of Terminology

Sorrow
A feeling of deep distress or pain caused by loss, disappointment, or other misfortune suffered by oneself or others.

Spousal Grief
Emotional pain, stress, depression, anxiety, grief, and loneliness felt due to the death of someone married, a significant other, or a life partner (CPA, 2005).

Stigma
A mark of shame or discredit (Merriam Webster, 2006).

Stigmatized Grief
Experiences and feelings of shame, blame, hopelessness, distress, coupled with profound sadness, and reluctance to seek or accept help during and after a traumatic grief/loss. Usually felt by survivors of gun violence death.

Stressors
Events or conditions that may cause physiological and behavioural reactions causing difficulties coping with distress.

Stress Reaction
The physiological and behavioural responses to stressors, including fatigue, high blood pressure, anger, and psychological distress.

Stuck-ness
A situation where the natural progression of the grieving process appears to be halted after a year. Usually described as being "stuck in grief."

Subtle Loss

Situations that cause separation from people, places, or things that are a part of one's life.
Although it is not always death, the separation causes emotional distress and loss of association.

Examples of Subtle Losses

- moving away from home
- migrating to another country
- getting laid off or losing a job
- losing a pet
- losing a friendship
- losing a piece of jewelry
- separation or divorce
- leaving home to attend university
- losing hair, a body part, or function
- selling a family home
- losing a sense of safety
- losing youth (ageing, balding, losing teeth)

Support System

A generic term referring to the extent and quality of an individual's social resources.

Survivor's Guilt

Emotions of remorse and self-blame, expressed by survivors who often felt that if they had been there or had done something differently, they might have been able to prevent the death of their loved one (OOB G-Social Group, 2019).

S.T.U.G.

Subsequent Temporary Upsurges of Grief (**S.T.U.G.**) is the sudden onset of traumatic pain from a loss, usually brought through the senses of sight, smell, touch, hearing and feeling.

T

Tears
The clear, salty, watery flow from the tear duct in the eyes. Usually is a spontaneous reaction to grief and trauma.

Thanatology:
The description or study of death and of psychological mechanisms for coping with loss.

Thanatophobia
Commonly referred to as the fear of death or fear of the dying process. Although it's most common in older adults, youth and younger children also experience thanatophobia, also recognized as "death anxiety" (Healthline, 2020).

Therapy
The treatment of mental or psychological disorders by psychological means—body, mental, or behavioural disorder (CPA, 2009).

Trained Facilitator
A person educated in the grieving process, grief/trauma support, who functions in a way that allows participants to assume responsibility for their unique learning and healing.

Trauma
An emotional shock following a stressful event, physical injury, or death. It may also be associated with physical shock and sometimes leads to long-term psychological distress.

Trauma-Focused Care
Based on knowledge of the impact of trauma, an approach aimed at ensuring environments and services are welcoming,

engaging, and customized for recipients and staff. Also referred to as Trauma-informed care.

Trauma-Focused Training
A specific approach to training, highlighting how traumatic incidents occur and prescribing care. It recognizes and emphasizes understanding how **traumatic** experiences impact mental, behavioural, emotional, physical, and spiritual wellbeing.

Trauma-Informed
Being trauma-informed means to:
    a) Possess acquired knowledge of foundational trauma
    b) Recognize the prevalence of adverse human experiences
    c) Understand that many behaviours and symptoms are the results of traumatic experiences
    d) Recognize that being treated with respect and kindness—and being empowered with choices—are critical factors in helping people recover from traumatic experiences
    e) Realize that the goal of trauma-informed care is to avoid re-traumatizing someone
    (Substance Abuse and Mental Health Services Administration SAMSHA, 2011)

Trauma-Troopers
People affected by trauma continue to persevere 'soldier on;' to function despite the magnitude of pain they are suffering or experiencing (OOB's Training, 2008).

Glossary of Terminology

Traumatic Grief
A type of grief characterized by suffering the death of a significant person under traumatic circumstances (e.g., accidents, an unexpected illness, homicide, **gun violence,** suicide, natural and human-made disasters, including experiencing or witnessing the death during horrific or life-threatening circumstances).

Trigger/s
Sudden, unexpected, and emotional reminders producing waves of intensely painful emotions. Triggers are associated with, and motivated by the senses—sight, sound, touch, feel, and smell.

Tunnel of Grief
Elizabeth Kubler-Ross used the tunnel as a metaphor for the grieving processes, stating that the only way through "the tunnel"—the grieving process—is by going through and that "healing comes when you realize that the light at the end of the tunnel is not a train."

U

Uncomplicated Grief
Although painful, normal grief reactions help move the survivor towards accepting the loss and carrying on with their life.

Under-Privileged
Having less money, education, etc., than the other people in a society; being poor and disadvantaged; having fewer advantages, privileges, and opportunities than most people.

Under-Served
To offer or provide inadequate services or facilities to specific neighbourhoods or people from a different culture.

Unresolved Grief
Considered to be the same as 'complex' or 'complicated grief.' It is characterized by the extended duration of symptoms that instills suicidal thoughts or actions; much more severe and intense, not lessening with time but getting increasingly worse. It lasts much longer, sometimes for many years; and, interferes with a person's ability to perform regular ADL (activities of daily life).

Upheaval
Emotions generated from the sudden death of a loved one. It can include but is not limited to anger, anxiety, apathy, feeling tearful, low mood, a sense of losing control, excitement, hopefulness, isolation, hopelessness, and withdrawal.

V

Violence
The intentional use of physical force or power, threatened or actual, against oneself, another person, or against a group or community that results in or has a high likelihood of injury, death, psychological harm, mal-development, or deprivation (WHO, 2002).

W

Weep
To express grief, sorrow, or any overpowering emotion by shedding tears. To utter or shed tears (Oxford Dictionary, 2010).

Weepies
Spontaneous and uncontrollable crying at the thought, mention of, or when speaking about a dead loved one.

Y

Yearning
An emotional state widely experienced in situations involving loss, with a focused desire for the person who was treasured.

Youth
Defined as the early stage in natural growth and development of young people (both sexes), between the periods of childhood to adulthood. Youth are usually between ages 15 to 24, but the age can be up to 26 years in marginalized communities.

Youth-Centric
An approach where youth are meaningfully engaged in programs and processes that spicificaly relates to them.

Youth-Engagement
Empowering all young people as valuable partners in addressing and making decisions about issues that affect them personally. Allowing youth to participate in all aspects of programs designed for and with youth in mind, including planning and implementation, evaluation, building partnerships, communication, and governance.

Z

Zig-Zag Trail
A course shaped like a 'Z,' typifying the grieving process, with abrupt, sharp turns and angles, including alternate right and left turns.

REFERENCES

Akers, Michael, & Porter, Grover. (2018). What is Emotional Intelligence (EQ)? https://psychcentral.com/lib/what-is-emotional-intelligence-eq/ Retrieved Dec. 3, 2018.

Allen, Britany, & Waterman, Helen. (2019). Stages of Adolescence. American Academy of Pediatrics. https://www.healthychildren.org/English/ages-stages/teen/Pages/Stages-of-Adolescence.aspx. Retrieved, Apr. 17, 2019.

Alexander, D. A., & Klein, S. (2005). The Psychological Aspects of Terrorism: From Denial to Hyperbole. Journal of the Royal Society of Medicine, 98(12), 557-562. DOI: 10. 1228/jrsm.98.12.557.

Armstrong, M., Carlson, J. Speaking of Trauma: the race talk, the gun violence talk, and the racialization of gun trauma. *Palgrave Commun* **5,** 112 (2019). https://doi.org/10.1057/s41599-019-0320-z. Retrieved Oct. 19, 2019.

Bailey, A., **Starr, S**., Lapum, J., & Akhtar, M. (2015). A Community-Based Model of Gun-Violent Traumatic Grief Support. *Journal of Advances in Social Science and Humanities*, 1(4).

Bailey, A., **Starr, S.** (2015). Women's Mental Health: Resistance and Resilience in Community and Society, Response, Springer, International Publishing Switzerland 2015. N. Khanlou, FB. Pilkington (eds.)

Bailey, A., Akhtar, M., & Clarke, J., **Sky Starr**. (2015). Intersecting Individual, Social and Cultural Factors in Black Mothers' Resilience-Building Following Loss to Gun Violence in Canada. In N. Khanlou & B. Pilkington (Eds., 311-325). Women's Mental Health: Resistance and Resilience in Community and Society. Springer International Publishing.

Bauger, Robert. (1997). A Guide to Understanding Guilt During Bereavement. Caring People Press.

Black Death / Plague. (n.d.) *"In Wikipedia."* Retrieved, Nov. 16, 2009, https://en.wikipedia.org/wiki/Black_Death. 27 June 2021.

Bradford John, & Townsend, Aubrey. (1843 & 2005,) *The Writings of John Bradford: Containing Letters, Treatises, Remains (Parker Society).*

Browning, Robert (1915). *Along The Road*. Journal of Education, https://journals.sagepub.com/ doi/10.1177/002205741508100315, Retrieved December 6, 2020.

Buchanan, Cate. (2014). Gun Violence, Disability and Recovery. Sydney: Surviving Gun Violence Project. Xlibris, Bloomington.

Busso, D. S., McLaughlin, K. A., & Sheridan, M. A. (01). Media Exposure and Sympathetic Nervous System Reactivity Predict PTSD Symptoms after the Boston Marathon Bombings. Depression and Anxiety, 31(7), 551-558. DOI: 10.1002/da.22282.

C.A.A. Savastano Quotes. (n.d.). Assessment Quotes. Retrieved January 14, 2021, from https://www.goodreads.com/quotes/tag/assessment.

Carper TL, Mills MA, Steenkamp MM, Nickerson A, Salters-Pedneault K, Litz BT. Early PTSD Symptom Sub-Clusters Predicting Chronic Posttraumatic Stress Following Sexual Assault. Psychological Trauma. 2015 Sep;7(5):442-7. DOI: 10.1037/tra0000060. Epub 2015 Jun 29. PMID: 26121173.

Crawford, Dorothy. (2018). *Deadly Companions: How Microbes Shaped Our History*. Oxford University Press.

Cicero, Marcus Tullius Quotes. (n.d.). BrainyQuote.com. Retrieved April 23, 2020, from BrainyQuote.com Web site: https://www.goodreads.com/quotes/6199-friendship-improves-happiness-and-abates-misery-by-doubling-our-joys.

City of Toronto Ward Profiles. (2016 Census). Ward 7 – Humber Black Creek, 2018 Profile, City of Toronto.

References

Dabbah, Mariela. (2014). What Is Cultural Sensitivity: In human Resources Management? Red Shoe Movement, https://redshoemovement.com/what-is-cultural-sensitivity/ Retrieved, June 15, 2019.

Declaration of Geneva. (2006). The Declaration of Geneva was adopted by the General Assembly of the World Medical Association at Geneva in 1948, amended in 1968, 1983, 1994, editorially revised in 2005 and 2006 and amended in 2017. https://en.wikipedia.org/wiki/Declaration_of_Geneva Retrieved July 2017.

de Guerre, Marc. (2018). CBC Docs POV's *Year of the Gun*, https://www.cbc.ca/cbcdocspov/episodes/year-of-the-gun Friday, March 8, 2019, 9 PM on CBC-TV. Retrieved March 27, 2019.

Duthie, Roger & Seils, Paul. (2017). Justice Mosaics: How Context Shapes Transitional Justice in Fractured Societies. International Centre for Transitional Justice. Research Report.

Eisma, Maarten C et al., "ICD-11 Prolonged Grief Disorder Criteria: Turning Challenges Into Opportunities With Multiverse Analyses." *Frontiers in psychiatry* vol. 11 752. 7 Aug. 2020, doi:10.3389/fpsyt.2020.00752.

Espada, Martin. (2006). Can Poetry Console a Grieving Public? https://www.poetryfoundation.org/features/articles/detail/68670. Retrieved, September 2007.

Eyerman, Ron. (2019). Memory, Trauma and Identity, Cultural Sociology, Palgrave Macmillan, 1st ed.

Freeman, Alan. (October 22, 2020). When it comes to Gun Control in Canada, the Minority Rules. iPOLITICS.

Viktor E. Frankl and Gordon W. Allport. (2000). Man's Search for Meaning, Beacon Press; 4th edition (March 30, 2000).

Garbarino, James et al., (2002). Mitigating the Effects of Gun Violence on Children and Youth.

Garbarino James. (2019) https://www.youtube.com/watch?v=RM6XXOsZZRk.

Gardner, Howard. (1999). Intelligence Reframed. Multiple intelligence for the 21st Century, New York: Basic Books.

Georgi, Anat. (2020). From Black Death to COVID-19: Science Advances, the Fear Remains. Pandemics elicit consistent human behaviour – hysteria and fear of others, HAARETZ, 03.20.20. https://www.haaretz.com/world-news/.premium.MAGAZINE-from-black-death-to-covid-19-science-advances-the-fear-remains-1.8691990. Retrieved, Mar. 16, 2020.

Gillespie, Claire. (2020). What Is Generational Trauma? Here's How Experts Explain It.

Goleman, Daniel. (2017). Daniel Goleman and his Theory on Emotional Intelligence. Exploring Your Mind. Dec. 27, 2017. https://exploringyourmind.com/daniel-goleman-and-his-theory-on-emotional-intelligence/. Retrieved, Feb. 12, 20108.

Government of Canada. (2021). Emergency Preparedness Guide, https://www.getprepared.gc.ca/cnt/rsrcs/pblctns/yprprdnssgd/index-en.aspx. Retrieved June 3, 2021.

Government of Canada. (2009). Mental Health – Depression, https://www.canada.ca/en/health-canada/services/healthy-living/your-health/diseases/mental-health-depression.html#ba. Retrieved, January 6, 2020.

Granek, L. & Peleg-Sagy, T. (2015). The Use of Pathological Grief Outcomes in Bereavement Studies on African Americans. Transcult Psychiatry. 2017 Jun; 54(3):384-399. DOI: 10.1177/1363461517708121. Retrieved, Feb 10, 2018.

Guarino, Ben. (2018). The Washington Post, Jan.16, 2018, at 4:25 p.m. EST. The Classic Explanation for the Black Death plague is wrong, scientists say. Retrieved, Jan 26, 2019.

Hardiman ER, Jones LV, Cestone LM. Neighbourhood Perceptions of Gun Violence and Safety: Findings from a Public Health-Social Work Intervention. Soc Work Public Health. 2019;34(6):492-504. DOI: 10.1080/19371918.2019.1629144. Epub 2019 Jun 26. PMID: 31241006.

Healthline, (2017). 9 Ways Crying May Benefit Your Health. https://www.healthline.com/health/benefits-of-crying. Retrieved December 2020.

"Hysteria." Web. June 17, 2020. https://www.vocabulary.com/dictionary/hysteria Retrieved, June 17, 2020.

Institute for Work and Health, (2015).

Janhevich, Bania, & Hastings. (2008). Rethinking Newcomer and Minority - Statistics Canada, (2012). Retrieved Jan. 20, 2018.

John of the Cross. (1578-1591). *"In Wikipedia."* https://en.wikipedia.org/wiki/John_of_the_ Cross. Last edited on June 3, 2021. Retrieved Sept. 17, 2020.

Kaufman, Scott Barry. (2020). Post-Traumatic Growth: Finding Meaning and Creativity in Adversity. https://blogs.scientificamerican.com/beautiful-minds/post-traumatic-growth-finding-meaning-and-creativity-in-adversity/ Retrieved September 12, 2020.

References

Keynes, John Maynard (1936). (n.d.) "*In Wikipedia.*" The General Theory of Employment, Interest and Money. *The Keynesian Multiplier Theory.* Retrieved, Nov. 16, 2009, https://en.wikipedia.org/wiki/Multiplier_(economics).

Kessler, R. C., Sonnega, A., Bromet, E., Hughes, M., Nelson, C. B., & Breslau, N. N. (1999). Epidemiological Risk Factors for Trauma and PTSD. In R. Yehuda (Ed.), Risk factors for PTSD. (pp. 23–59). Washington, DC: American Psychiatric Press.

Khanlou, Nazilla, Puikington, F, Beryl (editors, 2015). Women's Mental Health: Resistance and Resilience in Community and Society, Springer International Publishing.

Kimhi, S., & Shamai, M. (2004). Community Resilience and the Impact of Stress: Adult Response to Israel's Withdrawal from Lebanon. *Journal of Community Psychology, 32*(4), 439-451.

King, Martin Luther (1967). "Beyond Vietnam: *A Time to Break Silence.*" April 4th, 1967, http://www.ssc.msu.edu/~sw/mlkbrksInc.htm Retrieved, June 16, 2020. BRC-NEWS: Black Radical Congress - International News/Alerts/Announcements.

King, Martin Luther. (1963). Letter from Birmingham Jail, (1963). https://www.britannica.com/biography/Martin-Luther-Kinh-Jr/Legacy. Retrieved, May 6th, 2020.

Kounin, Jacob S. & Gump, Paul V. (Dec. 1958). The Elementary School Journal, Vol. 59, No. 3 pp. 158-162 Published by: The University of Chicago Press Stable URL: http://www.jstor.org/stable/999319. Accessed: 21/03/2013 09:57

Krug et al., (2002). "World Report on Violence and Health" Archived 2015-08-22 at the Wayback Machine, World Health Organization, 2002.

Latalova, Klara et al., (2014). "Perspectives on Perceived Stigma and Self-stigma in Adult Male Patients with Depression." *Neuropsychiatric disease and treatment* vol. 10 1399-405. 29 Jul. 2014, doi:10.2147/NDT.S5408. Retrieved, June 8, 2019.

Leibbrand C, Rivara F, Rowhani-Rahbar A. Gun Violence Exposure and Experiences of Depression among Mothers. Prev Sci. 2021 May;22(4):523-533. DOI: 10.1007/s11121-020-01202-7. Epub 2021 Jan 13. PMID: 33439439; PMCID: PMC7805261.

Leiner, M., Peinado, J., Villanos, M.T. Lopez, I., Uribe, R., & Pathak, (2016). Mental and Emotional Health of Children Exposed to News Media of Threats and Acts of Terrorism: The Cumulative and Pervasive Effects. *Frontiers in Pediatrics,* 4, 26. DOI: 10.3389/fped.2016.00026.

Link, Bruce, G. & Phelan, Jo C. (2001). Columbia University and New York State Psychiatric Institute. Annual Review of Sociology, Vol.27:363-385 (Volume publication date August 2001). https://doi.org/10.1146/annurev.soc.27.1.363. Retrieved, June 6, 2020.

Lynch, Peter. (2013). The Science Behind the Ripples and Wales in Water. The Irish Times, Thu, May 26, 2013, 02:00. https://www.irishtimes.com/news/science/the-science-behind-the-ripples-and-wakes-in-water-1.1394676. Retrieved, Jan 16, 2019.

Malti Tina, (2017). Severe Youth Violence: Developmental Perspectives Introduction to the Special Section. Child Development, Volume88, Issue 1; Pages 5-15; January/February 2017. https://srcd.onlinelibrary.wiley.com/doi/abs/10.1111/cdev.12694. Retrieved, January 10, 2018.

McCarthy-Jones, (2017). The Conversation, 'Sensing the dead is perfectly normal – and often helpful.' https://theconversation.com/sensing-the-dead-is-perfectly-normal-and-often-helpful-81048. Retrieved, Aug. 3, 2021.

McKaffery, Anne. (1997). Dragonsinger, (Harper Hill of Pern #2), 2003.

McLeod, Saul. (2018). Maslow's Hierarchy of Needs, Psychology Today, *Psychological Review, 50*(4), 370-96. Retrieved August 15, 2019.

McMurtry, R. & Curling, A. (2008). The Review of the Roots of Youth Violence. http://www.children.gov.on.ca/htdocs/English/professionals/oyap/roots/index.aspx. Retrieved November 20, 2008.

Medical Officer of Health, (Oct. 23, 2019). Community Violence in Toronto: A Public Health Approach – Report For Action HL11.1. https://www.toronto.ca/legdocs/mmis/2019/hl/bgrd/backgroundfile-139315.pdf. Retrieved October 30, 2019.

National Geographic, Common Octopus, (2014/090. http://ngm.nationalgeographic.com/2014/09/wilderness-act/kolbert-text. Retrieved, February 16, 2020.

National Police Federation, (Nov. 27, 2020). Position Statement, https://npfcontent.ca/wp-content/uploads/2020/11/Gun-Violence-and-Public-Safety-in-Canada-PS-Final-EN.pdf. Retrieved, December 11, 2020.

Neria Y., & Sullivan, G. M. (2011). Understanding the Mental Health Effects of Indirect Exposure to Mass Trauma through the Media, *Journal of the American Medical Association,* 306(12). 2374-1375. DOI: 10.1001/jama.2011.1358.

O'Donohoue, John. (1997). Anam Cara: A Book of Celtic Wisdom, New York: Cliff Street Books.

References

Oliver, Manuel, (2018). How a Father Deals With Loss After the Parkland Shooting. https://www.youtube.com/watch?v=PMFWWK_M-c. Retrieved December 3, 2018.

Papazoglou, Konstantinos et al., "Inevitable Loss and Prolonged Grief in Police Work: An Unexplored Topic." *Frontiers in psychology* vol. 11 1178. 29 May. 2020, doi:10.3389/fpsyg.2020.01178.

Park, C. L., & Folkmanm, S. (1997). Meaning in the Context of Stress and Coping. Review of General Psychology, 1,115-144. DOI: 10.1037/10889-2680.1.2.115.

Papazoglou, Konstantinos et al., "Inevitable Loss and Prolonged Grief in Police Work: An Unexplored Topic." *Frontiers in psychology* vol. 11 1178. 29 May. 2020, doi:10.3389/fpsyg.2020.01178.

Patel, Sonny S et al., "What Do We Mean by 'Community Resilience'? A Systematic Literature Review of How it is Defined in the Literature." *PLoS currents* vol. 9 ecurrents.dis.db775aff25efc5ac4f0660ad9c9f7db2. 1 Feb. 2017, doi:10.1371/currents.dis.db775aff25efc5ac4f0660ad9c9f7db2.

Pearlman, L. A., & Saakvitne, K. W. (1995). Trauma and the Therapist: Countertransference and Vicarious Traumatization *in Psychotherapy with Incest Survivors*. W. W. Norton & Co.

Plato's Theory of the Soul, *Wikipedia*, Wikimedia Foundation, March 28, 2021. https://en.wikipedia.org/wiki/Plato%27s_theory_of_soul. Retrieved November 6, 2020.

Porges, Stephen., Ogden, Pat., Siegel, Dan., Lanius, Riuth., van Der Kolk, Bessel., (2020). The National Institute for the Clinical Application of Behavioural Medicine (NICABM).

Preeti, Aroon (2007). The Ripple Effect of the Iraq War, Foreign Policy- the Global Magazine of News and Ideas. hppts://www.bing.com/search?FORM=SLBRDF&PC=SL10&q=FP+News. Retrieved, April 10, 2019.

Proncea Becker, Joanna & Quartilho, Manuel, Joao, (April 2021). Colonial War: When the Years Rekindle the Suffering – A Pilot Study. Darío Acuña-Castroviejo, Editor, *Reports* 2021, 4(2), 10; https://doi.org/10.3390/reports4020010. Retrieved, May 11, 2021.

Saunders, Natasha R., Lee, Hannah, Macpherson, Alison, Guan, Jun, and Guttmann, Astrid. (2017). CMAJ March 27, 2017, 189 (12) E452-E458; DOI: https://doi.org/10.1503/cmaj.160850. Retrieved Jan. 10, 2019.

Shakespeare, William. (1967). Measure for Measure, (Arden Shakesoeare: Swcond Series) (1604) act 3, sc. 1, 1. 2. J. W. Lever (Editor).

Shakespeare, William. (1623). As You Like It, (Arden Shakespeare: Third Series (1998), act 2, sc, 5, Dover Publications.

Smith Lee, Jocelyn R. (2015). Who Gets to Be a Victim of Gun Violence? Examining the Marginalized R=Trauma and Greif of Boys and Men in Black Families.

Smith, J. R. (2015). Unequal Burdens of Loss: Examining the Frequency and Timing of Homicide Deaths Experienced by Young Black Men across the Life Course. *American Journal of Public Health*, 105(S3), S483–S490. doi:10.2105/AJPH.2014.302535.

Starr, Sky. (2015). Response – Intersecting Individual, Social and Cultural Factors in Black Mothers Resilience Building Following Loss to Gun Violence in Canada.

Statistics Canada. (2016). Statistics Canada, Canadian Centre for Justice Statistics, Uniform Crime Reporting Survey. http://www.statcan.gc.ca/pub/85-002-x/2017001/article/54879-eng.htm. Retrieved Jan. 12, 2019).

Staughton, John. (7 Feb. 202). Water Ripples: What Causes Ripples in Water? https//www.scienceabc.com/eyeopeners/what-causes-ripple-in-water.html. Retrieved, may 24, 2020.

Stroebe, Margaret. Boerner, Kathrin. In International Encyclopedia of the Social & Behavioural Sciences (Second Edition), 2015. Retrieved, November 12, 2020.

Strobe, Margaret et al., "Guilt in Bereavemnet: the Role of Self-Blame and Regret in Coping with Loss." *PloS one* vol. 9,5 e966906. 12 May. 2014, doi: 10.1371/journal.pone.0096606.

Sullivan, C.P., Smith, A. J., Lewis, M., & Jones, R. T. (2018). Network Analysis of PTSD Symptoms following Mass Violence. *Psychological Trauma: Theory, Research, Practice, and Policy, 10*(1), 58-66. https//doiorg/10.1037/tra0000237.

Thompson, S. K. (2014). Case Study: Black Homicide Victimization in Toronto, Ontario, Canada. In S. M. Bucerius & M. Tony (Eds.), *Oxford handbook of ethnicity, crime, and immigration*. Toronto ON: Oxford UP.

Toronto Police Service, (2018). Public Safety Data Portal, TPS Crime Statistics – Shootings, http://data.torontopolice.on.ca/pages/shootings. Retrieved Jan. 12, 2019.

References

Toronto Police Service, (2021). Homicide Cold Cases. https://www.torontopolice.on.ca/homicide/coldcases.php. Retrieved, May 5, 2021.

UNODC, (2019). United Nations Office on Drugs and Crime. Global Study on Homicide 2019 (Vienna, 2019).

Van der Kolk, B. (2000). Posttraumatic Stress Disorder and the Nature of Trauma. Dialogues in Clinical Neuroscience 2 (1), 7-22.

Van Biema, David, (2007). Mother Teresa's Crisis of Faith. https://time.com/4126238/mother-teresas-crisis-of-faith/. August 23, 2007. Retrieved, June 22, 2021.

Van der Kolk, B. A. (2014). *The Body Keeps the Score: Brain, Mind, and Body in the Healing of Trauma.* Viking.

Violence Policy Center, (2017). The Relationship between Community Violence and Trauma: How Violence Affects Learning, Health, and Behaviour. https://vpc.org/studies/trauma17.pdf Retrieved October 26, 2019.

Vollman, Ardene Robinson, Jackson, Susan, F. (5th Ed., 2021). Canadian Community as Partner: Theory and Multidisciplinary Practice, Fourth Edition, Wolters Kluwer, (451-460).

Vollman, E.T. Anderson, J.M. McFarlane (4th ed., chap. 37). Canadian Community as Partner: Theory & Multidisciplinary Practice. Wolters Kluwer.

Weiston-Serdan, Torie. (2017). Critical Mentoring: A Practical Guide, Stylus Publishing. WHO (2005) Moving Beyond the Tsunami: The WHO Story, Chapter 4. *The Lessons Learnt*, 2005.

Wesley, John Quotes. (n.d.). BrainyQuote.com. Retrieved April 20, 2020, from BrainyQuote.com Web site: https://www.brainyquote.com/quotes/john_wesley_524889.

William J. Winslade, et al., (2006). Frankl, Victor, E. Man's Search for Meaning (first) Edition.

World Health Organization - WHO. (2017). 10 Facts About Violence Prevention.

World Health Organization - WHO (2016, September 30). Youth Violence. https://www.who.int/news-room/fact-sheets/detail/youth-violence. Retrieved May 7, 2017.

World Health Organization - WHO (2005) Moving Beyond the Tsunami: The WHO Story, Chapter 4. *The Lessons Learnt*, 2005.

World Health Organization – WHO (2020, June 8, 20). Youth Violence. https://www.who.int/news-room/fact-sheets/detail/youth-violence. Retrieved January 6, 2021.

Zaki, Jamil. (2019, 2020). The War for Kindness: Building Empathy in a Fractured World. New York, NY: Penguin Random House.

Zisook, Sidney, and Katherine Shear. "Grief and Bereavement: What Psychiatrists Need to Know." *World psychiatry:official journal of the World Psychiatric Association (WPA)* vol. 8,2 (2009): 67-74. doi:10.1002/j.2051-5545.2009.tb00217.x.

Ravisky@outofbonds.jj.or
Hi 437 3079
Blod 427 3079

Made in the USA
Monee, IL
10 September 2023

42415503R00151